GOD'S
EXISTENCE:
RELIGIOUS AND SCIENTIFIC REFLECTION

RAVI K. PURI, Ph.D.

authorHOUSE

AuthorHouse™
1663 Liberty Drive
Bloomington, IN 47403
www.authorhouse.com
Phone: 833-262-8899

Published by AuthorHouse 12/05/2022

ISBN: 978-1-6655-7691-8 (sc)
ISBN: 978-1-6655-7692-5 (hc)
ISBN: 978-1-6655-7693-2 (e)

Contents

Dedication ix

About the Author xi

Acknowledgment xiii

Thoughts Create Reality xv

Preface..xvii

Chapter One   Inner Quest to Know God 1

Chapter Two   Origin and Evolution of God 6

Chapter Three   Concept of God in Different Religions....................... 16

Chapter Four   Eminent Scientists: Believers in God.................30

Chapter Five   Eminent Scientists: Nonbelievers in God....................39

Chapter Six   Celebrities: Nonbelievers in God................................46

Chapter Seven   Concept of Heaven and Hell.......................................53

Chapter Eight   Is there Life after Death?...66

Chapter Nine   Reincarnation and Karma..75

Chapter Ten   God's Existence: Religion Reflection 83

Chapter Eleven   Creation of the Universe: Religion Reflection 91

Chapter Twelve   Creation of the Universe: Scientific Reflection......... 101

Chapter Thirteen   The Creator and The Universe................................. 107

Chapter Fourteen   God's Existence & the Kardashev Scale.................. 115

Chapter Fifteen   The Quest for the Unknown 125

Afterword... 133

Bibliography... 135

Glossary of Terms... 141

Before the Universe

"Neither existence nor nonexistence was there. There was neither the realm of space nor the sky beyond.
But for that breathless one breathing on its own. There was nothing else, surely nothing.
Darkness was hidden by darkness in the beginning, with no distinguishing.
In the beginning, all this verily was Atman (Supreme Being) only.
For Om, the five elements came to be; space, air (gas), fire (plasma), water (liquid), and earth (Solid)."

— Rig Veda (8:129)

Where is God?

"I looked for God. I went to a temple and I didn't find him there. Then I went to a church and I didn't find him there. Then I went to a mosque and I didn't find him there. Then finally I looked in my heart and there he was."

— <u>Rumi</u>

Dedication

To my wife Mrinal Puri who will always remain my inspiration. There is not any moment that I let her go from my thoughts.

—Ravi K. Puri

"Without you, I feel lonely in this crowded world."

About the Author

D r. Ravi K. Puri has served his profession for almost thirty years in teaching and research. He has a broad range of experience and excelled in the field of Pharmacy, Biochemistry, and Environmental sciences. He has taught and researched at various renowned Universities in the USA and abroad. He has published nearly a hundred research papers and scientific reviews in journals of international repute including chapters in reference books published by CRC Press and Lewis publishers. He has been on the review panels of many prestigious scientific journals in the USA and abroad.

He took early retirement from the University of Missouri while working as a Group Leader at the Environmental Trace Research Center and joined the hospitality industry in 2000. He also excelled in hospitality because of his arduous work and honesty. Today, the Puri Group of Hospitality is enjoying an excellent reputation in the state of Missouri, USA, and has international franchises like Hilton Garden Inn, Double Tree, Holiday Inn, Hampton Inn, and Comfort Suites along with restaurants like Garden Grill, Sapphire, and a couple of Cheerleader Grills.

He is the celebrated author of the book entitled *Natural Aphrodisiac: Myth or Reality.* The book is widely acclaimed by physicians, pharmacists, nurses, natural products chemists, and herbalists. It is one of the most comprehensive and informative compilations on Natural Aphrodisiacs.

Apart from being a scientist, he has also been practicing spirituality. He has already published a book entitled *Consciousness: The Ultimate Reality.* Many readers highly applauded the book. Recently, he wrote another book, *Meditation Over Medication* which was also highly acclaimed by the readers. The present publication is the result of his continuing search and belief in spirituality.

> *"God is an intelligent sphere,*
> *whose center is everywhere, and*
> *whose circumference is nowhere".*
> *— Hermes Trismegistus*

Acknowledgment

First, I am extremely grateful to my consciousness who is the real author of this book. I sincerely offer my humble gratitude from the core of my heart to 'That' existence who gave me the strength and intellect to express my feelings. I could sense that invisible power directing, assisting, and protecting me during the various walks of my life. I am honestly indebted to 'That'.

My gratitude to all my circumstances for compelling me to write on this topic. My wife Mrinal passed away after I published my previous book *Meditation Over Medication*. Her departure changed my life dramatically. I could never imagine that she was a potential source of my life and that all my activities revolved around her. She had been a great source of inspiration for my progress and achievements in my life. Her parting was a great shock to me. I was unable to continue and concentrate on my writing. I decided not to write again. In the middle of these circumstances, Sue Chen of The Regency Publishers encouraged me to write this text. She has been consistent in her efforts and never stopped calling me now and then. Finally, she talked me into this. I am grateful to her. At the same time, it was a spiritual awakening for me to realize that I need to move on and hold fast to the present instead of dwelling in the past.

Ravi K. Puri, Ph.D.
Columbia, MO, USA

Thoughts Create Reality

Thoughts are immensely powerful and can drastically change the life of a person. Whatever thoughts, one carries in his or her mind will continue to influence the emotions, actions, and finally personality of that person. In other words, the entire alchemy of the body is changed through the thought process. What a person thinks that he becomes. What a man's mind dwells upon according to that his life and character are molded, along his destiny. As within, so without.

The belief system, feelings, emotions, and actions, if remain the same would bring the same stereotype of results again and again in the life of a person. "The definition of insanity is doing the same thing over and over again and expecting different results," was illustrated by Albert Einstein. If anyone wants different results, he must change the pattern of thinking. That would eventually transform an individual's feelings, emotions, actions, habits, and character. Controlling thoughts is not an easy phenomenon. The more you persist them, the more they resist. If you do not learn to control your thoughts, you will never learn to control your behavior. However, deviation of thoughts is possible. Please change the quality of your thoughts that will transform your destiny. Remember, *Thoughts become things*.

— The author

> *"The happiness of your life depends on the quality of your thoughts."*

Preface

The subject of the book has been very controversial and complicated since time immemorial. Scientists have been trying hard to prove the existence of God and all religions are working day and night to explain the presence of God from their holy scriptures. Science being objective wants solid proof of God's existence whereas religion being subjective believes in faith and professes that God is eternal and beyond time and space. Despite, all the debates, inquiries, discussions, and research so far, no concrete decision has been made on the existence of God. High-tech artificial intelligence is still in the race to explore and prove the presence of God.

Recently, Mark Zuckerberg, an American business magnate, internet entrepreneur, philanthropist, and co-founder of Facebook became a theist from an atheist. Antony Flew, a well-known British philosopher and staunch advocate of atheism changed his mind at the age of 80 despite having dedicated all his life to science. He wrote a book, *There is a God*. He believed in the existence of an intelligent creator. He became a theist. Likewise, Jorden Peterson, a Canadian Professor of Psychology, said he was not an atheist anymore.

John Carson Lennox, a Northern Irish mathematician, bioethicist, and author of many books on religion strongly admitted the existence of God.

On the other hand, Daniel Edwin Barker was an American atheist who served as an evangelical Christian preacher and composer for 19 years but left Christianity in 1984. Likewise, Richard Dawkins, a famous evolutionary biologist, and an atheist wrote the book, *The God Delusion*. The book proved to be New York Times bestseller. Michael Brant Shermer, an American science writer, once a fundamentalist Christian, ceased to believe in the existence of God. He considers himself a nontheistic, atheist, and skeptic. British theoretical physicist Stephen Hawking emphatically accepted that he was an atheist. Elon Musk, an American entrepreneur, investor, and business magnate, was not comfortable admitting God's existence when asked about his thoughts on God. Numerous scientists do not believe in the existence of God and at the same time, some noble laureates are believers in God.

Similarly, mystics like J.D. Krishnamurti, a philosopher, speaker, and writer; Osho, an Indian godman did not believe in the existence of the creator. Likewise, Sadguru, an Indian yoga guru, exponent of spirituality, and founder of the Isha Foundation does not support the existence of God.

I was perplexed to know how these legendary scientists and mystics change their concepts of the existence of God after practicing their philosophy for decades. There must be some solid reasons for their awakening. My inquisitiveness to explore the existence of God increased day by day. Finally, I decided to review the entire literature available on this topic and draw a conclusion including my experience on the existence of God, in the shape of this text. I hope the information collected and interpreted will benefit the readers struggling to find the ultimate truth about the existence of God.

"The cosmos is within us. We are made of star-stuff. We are a way for the universe to know itself"
—Carl Sagan

Chapter One
Inner Quest to Know God

"Ignite your Inner fire, explore it, and share it with the world."
—Ravi K. Puri.

I Was born into a religious family. Religious rituals were done regularly and we followed them with utmost care. A kind of fear was imbibed in the kids, if you do not practice prayers rightfully, you would be punished by God. Nevertheless, for going to class exams or playing any sport for competition, we were advised to pray to God for His blessings. God's permission and blessings were very important parts of our life during our childhood and even continued later on. The impressions, we were given about God as a superhuman being, who can solve our problems provided we pray to Him regularly.

My parents taught all the children, "God is omnipresent, omniscient, and omnipotent, you cannot hide anything from Him. He lives in the sky. He watches all your actions. If you are doing anything wrong such as lying, stealing, and cursing others. He is going to punish you. Bad deeds and actions will take you to hell and good deeds to heaven." They further explained to us the description of hell and heaven. This further scared us. This information, imbibed in me as well as in the other four siblings' fear, and curiosity to know Him who knows everything and who is present everywhere: powerful, unborn, immortal, self-illuminated, and invisible. The inner quest to know the unknown was ignited in me during my childhood. My mind was full of questions and self-inquiry was going on all the time.

I imagined Him as a big, powerful old man with a white beard, sitting on a throne enwrapped by clouds and speaking with a heavy voice. My curiosity to know him increased day by day. Questions started rolling in my thoughts.

Who is He? Where does He live? What type of house is He living in there in the sky? How can He live among the clouds? Is He alone?

Is He married? Does he have kids? Do they have shopping centers there? What kind of food is available there? Do they have trees and other vegetation there? How does He control the entire Universe? How does He travel? What kind of transportation does He have? Why is He living in the sky? What kind of person is He? Is He handsome and charming? Or ugly and cruel? Is he young or old? Do hell and heaven exist? Or it is an idea to steer us in the right direction.

These questions used to gnaw at me all the time. I was reluctant to ask these questions to my parents or teachers. I was afraid; they might consider me a fool or a crazy boy. The more a person thinks about God, the more complex and imaginative the concept becomes.

As I grew up, my quest to know the Almighty God was also enhanced. I started reading books about religion. I was born in a Hindu family, so it was easier for me to know first Hinduism. By the time I was 16, I read two critical religious books Bhagwat Gita and Ramayana. I was very much fascinated by Lord Krishna's life and his preaching through Bhagwat Gita. However, Ramayana was a story of Rama's life, and there were specific descriptions in the form of *Shlokas* that were beyond my comprehension. However, I learned from my mother how to read and recite the *shlokas* of Ramayana. My interest was more towards Bhagwat Gita which preached more than a religion. In my opinion, Gita is above religion, mostly spiritual.

My parents were living in a neighborhood predominantly a Sikh community. Most of our neighbors were Sikhs families. They influenced my childhood and adolescence. The back side of our house was a Sikh temple known as *Gurdwara*. Early at 4 am, the Sikh priest started singing sermons of the Sikh religion in the *Gurdwara*. While half-sleep, I could hear them. Sikhism teaches the philosophy of nonviolence and spiritualism. *Japji Sahib's* narration of Sikh Guru, Nanak Dev Ji impressed me a lot. It is a famous and concise philosophy described in praise of God.

Most of the population in my hometown was of the Jains community who believe in a religion known as Jainism. Some of my close friends were Jains. I got the opportunity to explore Jainism. The Jainism religion teaches non-violence, non-attachment, and asceticism. Jains take five main vows: *non-violence, truth, not stealing, celibacy* or *chastity or sexual continence*, and *non-attachment*. These principles have influenced Jain culture to a great extent such as leading to a predominantly vegetarian lifestyle that avoids harm to animals and their life cycles. Jainism has between four and five million followers, with most Jains residing in India only. Some of the largest Jain communities are present in Canada, Europe, Kenya, the United Kingdom, Hong Kong, Fiji, and the United States.

I liked one of the aspects of the Jain religion that *there was no beginning and no end to the Universe. Every realized soul is God.* However, there is one aspect about their Jain Gurus, walking naked, barefooted in the procession among young and old people wearing a mask around their mouths, which did not captivate me. Though, wearing a mask has become a way of life today.

After completing my post-graduate studies in pharmaceutical sciences, I joined my *alma mater* as an assistant professor in 1970. I taught there for ten years and remained busy with teaching and research, got little time to practice or follow any religion. I was awarded a post-doctorate fellowship for two years in 1980 to pursue research on anticancer drugs from plants at the University of Mississippi, Oxford, USA. After completing my fellowship, I decided to settle in the USA for better prospects for my sons and accepted a faculty position there.

During my stay in the United States, I was influenced by some Christian friends and studied the life and preaching of Jesus Christ, too. I liked and admired most The Christian teachings, particularly the Ten Commandments.

I had a Muslim Ph.D. student Neena Abraham from Sudan. After completing her Ph.D., she left for Abu Dhabi to join a faculty position. She gifted me a copy of the Holy Quran. I enjoyed exploring Quran, too. I always fail to understand why there is so much violence, unrest, and terrorism in Muslim countries when their Holy Quran teaches nonviolence. I was consoled by the expression of Bertrand Russell, a great British Philosopher expressed very deeply, "The whole problem with the world is that fools and fanatics are always so certain of themselves, and wiser people so full of doubts." After going through most of the religions and their philosophies, I found that the essence of all religions is virtually the same. Though, these differ in their practice and way of belief systems convey the same message. God is one, self-created, shapeless, birthless, ageless, deathless, omnipresent, self-illuminated whose perception is ineffable. All religions lead finally to one destination, as all rivers merge into one big ocean.

The questions baffled me all the time. *Why do people fight for different religions? Why do they hate each other for religion?* God has no religion. Religion is the concept of human beings and has been changing continuously with the mist of time. Religion is a belief or faith in any dogma or philosophy. Religion divides society whereas spirituality unites it. One can believe in anything whatever he feels comfortable with but should not criticize or curse any other religion or belief. Robert F. Kennedy articulated very precisely, "What is objectionable, what is dangerous about extremists is not that they are extreme, but that they are intolerant. The evil is not what they say about their cause, but what they say about their opponents."

Extreme belief or dogma in any concept generates anger, prejudice, and hate. Likewise, fanaticism in religion and discrimination in any race can adversely affect an individual, society, and, the entire nation in general.

Throughout the world, there are about 4300 recognized religions. Each one preaches and claims that his religion is the right and the best one. Spirituality is only one truth above the religions and sees the truth in all of them. It unites them because the truth is the same for all human beings despite their differences and uniqueness. It focuses on the quality of the divine message they share. Moreover, spirituality is related to the soul whereas religion is to the mind. Religion is the belief in someone's experience whereas spirituality is having its own experience. Religion creates fear and spirituality gives you freedom. Religion is a cult and spirituality is meditation. Religion lives in thoughts and spirituality lives in consciousness. Moreover, religion lives in the past, and future whereas spirituality lives in the present. Above all, spirituality begins where religion ends. Thus, spirituality is above religion. I started practicing spirituality instead of following one religion. I do not support any dogma or theology. To practice spirituality, there is no need for religion. However, one thing always nipping me about the *Existence of God*. If He is there then He should prevent deadly events comprising genocides, atrocities, and crimes.

During my search for the ultimate reality, I met many mystics and asked them about the existence of God. Everybody had a different concept of the existence of God as per his or her belief and experience. I could not get any satisfactory solution from any of them, rather they confused me. On the other hand, science could not prove or disprove the existence of God. Finally, I carried out my research on the Existence of God through religious and scientific reflection. This text is the outcome of my review, interpretation, and self-experience about the existence of God. I hope it will be beneficial to all of them who are interested to know Him.

"Religion is the sigh of the oppressed creature, the heart of a heartless world, and the soul of soulless conditions. It is the opium of the people."
—*Karl Max*

Chapter Two
Origin and Evolution of God

"The greatest untold story is the evolution of God."
— *G.I. Gurdjieff*

Before we discuss the existence of God, it is very pertinent to assimilate the concept of God, origin, and evolution. People of all ages and stages in life have contemplated the origin of God. Scientists and mystics are baffled and questioned the existence of God. Where does God come from? Is God real or a concept? Where was He before the beginning of time? Did He spontaneously appear? The answer is not easy, however, religion has the reply but there is no proof. According to religion, He was there even before time, space, and the Big Bang. It's faith without any evidence.

The concept of God came into the human mind as a powerful superhuman being who can solve their problems. That's why many skeptics or atheists consider God as man's creativity. They think weak-minded people believe in a higher being who listens to their prayers and acts on their behalf. The atheist theory is, if God can't be explained, He mustn't exist.

However, it is very relevant to know the term, *God*. The question arises, who coined the term, *God*? The exact origin of the word *God* is unknown. However, according to the literature, it is a European invention that was never used in any of the Judeo-Christian scriptures. People have been contending and fighting over the name of *God* for long though they do not know where the word *God* came from. Let us go back to the evolution of gods and religions. Humans started about 400,000 years ago. At that time, there was no communication among them except sign and sound language. Nevertheless, they were very ignorant about morals, ethics, and clothing. They expressed their basic needs of fear, hunger, or sex through sound and signs.

About one hundred thousand years ago, the race started interacting with each other with the invention of language. Man learned to speak and named objects and relations. The origin of the first language among humans is very interesting but unknown. No one knows for sure about the evolution of language. Who invented the alphabet? How did their sound come into existence? The origin of Zero and the concept of arithmetic and the writing of language are amazing evolution.

However, it is a separate topic and does not come in the present discussion. Anyway, communication change the destiny of humanity and they started sharing their emotions such as joy, sorrow, pain, and pleasure with broken dialogues, signs, sounds, and body language,

At some point in time, whenever people came across some natural power beyond their control that could harm them, they began to worship that natural power for help by folding their hands, bowing, kneeling, and praying to that power. For example, they used to get scared of thunderstorms and lightning and considered these an act of superpower in the sky. They started worshiping the sky. During winter and icy cold weather, they thought the sun was angry and not rising. They started worshiping the sun to rise and save them. Scared of earthquakes led them to worship the earth. Unstoppable rain and floods disaster compelled them to worship the rain god to end this catastrophe. The invention of fire by rubbing stones was considered an act of superpower so fire was considered the 'Fire god'. Similarly, tornados and storms were considered the act of superhuman power, to worship the wind. Hurricane in the seas was considered an act of the sea getting angry, worshipping the sea was a very common practice.

Where there is life, there is death. Soon the concept of the soul came to light and people realized that there was an *invisible divine spark* that provide life to a physical body. When that *divine spark* was no more in the body, it was called death. Thus, humans accepted the *existence* of superhuman power and started prayers or some kinds of rituals to worship that *superhuman power* or *existence* for their protection. Thus, a kind of religious activities were started with the idea that there was a metaphysical power or *divine power* behind all natural events. They started seeking some ways to pacify that divine power through prayers, supplication for mercy, dancing around the fire with gratifying songs, etc. These social activities were the beginning of the religious era and subsequently transmitted to the next progeny.

The superhuman powers were given different names in far-flung parts of the world as per their likings, dislikings, and traditions. In Hinduism, *Brahma* is usually considered a monistic concept of God. There are also many other names such as *Ishvara, Paramatta, Bhagwan,* and *Rabb* for God in different languages and dialects in India. *Waheguru* is used in Sikhism. In Chinese religion, *Shangdi* is perceived as the originator of the universe. In Hebrew, God comprises *Elohim*, and *Adonai* (Lord). The names *Yahweh* and *Jehovah*, are used in Christianity. In the Christian doctrine of the Trinity, one God includes three called the *Father, the Son, and the Holy Spirit.* In Islam, God *"Allah"* is frequently used as a name, while Muslims also have several other names. and *Ahura Mazda* in Zoroastrianism.

During this period, about 200,000 years back, people start carving on stones and wood the image of God and goddesses as per their imaginations. Slowly and steadily life improved.

With the evolution of civilization about 12000 years ago, temples were erected, and idols were installed. Regular visits and prayers were started in different parts of the earth's planet. The world's oldest temple suggests the urge to worship sparked civilization. Mann (2011) described in his article entitled, *The Birth of Religion, in national Geography*, a 11600-year-old temple of Gobekli Tepe in southern Turkey. The temple pillars are 18 feet tall and may represent priestly dancers at a gathering. The temple was built by hunter-gathers. The site is vaguely reminiscent of Stonehenge and made of cleanly carved limestone pillars. Animals like boar, crane, fox, scorpion, and snakes carved on the pillars are native to the area and may represent guardian spirits. It is the oldest known temple of monumental architecture. When these pillars were erected, nothing of comparable scale existed in the world. At the time of construction, many humans lived in small nomadic bands and survived on plants and hunting wild animals. Amazingly, the temple's builders were able to cut, shape and transport 16-ton stones hundreds of feet having no wheels. Archeologists are still excavating the Gobekli Tepe temple and doing further research on this unique temple. It is very appropriate to mention here that the 32000-year-old Lord Narasimha Hindu idol was discovered in Southern Germany in 1939. That means Hinduism is the world's oldest religion.

When the last blast of the Ice age ended about 10,000 years past. People responded to the warmer environment by focusing on agriculture which gave rise to organized religion. After people began setting in villages and farming, religion arose to promote social activities. People came together for rituals. The development of agriculture gave rise to cities and later to writing, art, and religion. Subsequently, the population started to increase. They started to live comfortably. Soon natural calamities like floods and droughts occurred which resulted in famine. People turned to God and goddesses for protection. Whenever they faced a new challenge, they started praying to God considering that God has created this problem and He is going to fix it. To please God and to get rid of natural calamities, they used to do all kinds of rituals and sacrifices at the places of worship.

Around 10,000 years ago, Hinduism came to light in the Indus Valley. It is also known as *Sanatan Dharma* meaning *Eternal Order* or *Eternal Path*. Vedas, the holy scriptures of Hinduism originated during this period. The Vedas are the oldest scriptures of Hinduism. They were derived from the ancient Indo-Aryan culture of the Indian Subcontinent and began as an oral tradition that was passed down through generations. Aryans developed Vedas, which comprise worship of natural elements such as the sun, sky, earth, rain, water, air, fire, land, and gods and goddesses. Thus, religious rituals and worship the supernatural powers became the way of life in Indian Subcontinent.

Almost 3000 years back, agriculture progressed, and farmers produced enough food. Permanent houses with stones were erected for protection from unfavorable weather. At the same time, farming gave rise to parasites like rodents, mosquitos, and houseflies which resulted in diseases. People began to cure the sick with the help of worship, rituals, magic, and herbs. Diseases were considered an act of demons at that time.

They started building places for worship all over the globe. Mundeshwari temple is considered the oldest temple in India which is located in Kaimur District, Bihar. It is still active, Archeological Survey of India has restored it and its construction probably dated back to 108 AD. The construction of temples in India dates to about 2000 years ago. There are 24 ancient temples built during the first century. The exact dates are not known since temples and their records were destroyed by Mughal invasions. Mughals intended to eradicate the Hindu religion and replace temples with mosques to promote Islam. Islamic rulers prevented Hindus from worshipping their deities. About forty thousand temples were destroyed and modified into mosques in India during the Mughal period.

The human population also started increasing which gave pave to social evils like poverty, injustice, crime, jealousy, and social inequality leading to miseries. Several great prophets and philosophers such as the Buddha, Hippocrates, Socrates, and Plato conceived the causes and remedies for human suffering around 2500 years ago. However, they also believed in metaphysical power.

Likewise, Buddha proposed that human sufferings were the cause of desires and punishment of the sinful karma committed in the previous life. He proposed certain morals ethics and meditation to get rid of them. His meditation techniques also pointed out some metaphysical power, God.

About 2000 years ago, Moses suggested the Ten Commandments, sacrifices, and prayers protect people from their miseries. Jesus asserted some morals and ethics sanctified with the metaphysical Power of the Father, the Son and the Holy Spirit. The concept of gathering in groups for worship was started by Jesus which later took the shape of the Church. The church is not a building but a group of people loving and glorifying God. The purpose of the church was to join people of different backgrounds and talents and provide them with training and opportunities for God's work. It accomplishes both internally, within the body, and externally, in the world.

Aryabhatt (476-550 CE) was a great Indian mathematician and astronomer. He worked on the place value system and discovered zero for the first time, making use of letters to indicate numbers and pointing out qualities. He discovered the position of nine planets and expressed that these likewise rotated around the sun. He explained the cause of the eclipses of the Sun and Moon. He gave the perfect value of the circumference of the Earth. Aryabhatt valued the length of the year as 365 days 6 hours 12 minutes and 30 seconds.

Nearby 1400 years ago, Prophet Muhammad came to light and initiated Islam by bifurcating it from Abraham's religion. Islam and Christianity religions quite similar to each other. As the Quran was being revealed in the 610 Common Era, the Prophet Muhammad made special arrangements to ensure that it was written down. Although the Prophet Muhammad himself could neither read nor write, he dictated the verses orally and instructed scribes to mark down the revelation on whatever materials were available. The scribes would then read their writing back to the Prophet, who would check it for mistakes.

Soon Johannes Gutenberg (1400-1468) designed the printing press. Knowledge is power, as the saying goes, and the invention of the mechanical movable type printing press helped disseminate knowledge wider and faster than ever before. German goldsmith Johannes Gutenberg was credited with inventing the printing press around 1436,

The Vedas were orally transmitted by memorization for many generations and were written down for the first time around 1200 BCE. Vedas were written in the Vedic Sanskrit language between 1500 and 500 BCE (Before Common Era). The Vedas comprise four texts and 108 Upanishads. The four Vedas are *Rig Veda*, *Sama Veda*, *Yajur Veda* and *Atharva Veda*. Out of 108 Upanishads, only 10 are the principal Upanishads: *Isha, Kena, Katha, Prashan, Mundaka, Mandukya, Tattiriya, Aitareya, Chhandogya, and Brihadaranyaka.*

However, all printed editions of the Vedas that survive in modern times are likely the version existing in about the 16th century AD.

The writings of religious books such as the Bible, Vedas, Koran, etc. started about 500 years back.

Galileo Galilei (1564-1642) surprised the people and philosophers of that time 500 years back, by inventing telescopes and the rotation and shape of the earth. The earth which used to be considered flat found to be round. Another miracle of nature about the earth being flat was cleared by the scientific invention. Giordano Bruno, an Italian philosopher, was burnt to death in 1600 CE because he refused to disown the theory that the earth goes around the sun. Imagine – he was brutally killed for stating the truth only 500 years ago. Though the earth was mentioned round in the Holy Scripture of Vedas about 5000 years ago.

Louis Pasteur (1822-1895) a French chemist and microbiologist renowned for his discoveries of the principles of vaccination, microbial fermentation, and pasteurization discovered that microbes were responsible for causing diseases, not the demon. His discoveries about anthrax and rabies vaccination saved thousands of lives.

Alexander Fleming (1881-1955) Scottish physician and microbiologist discovered Penicillin. His discovery and use of Penicillin have saved millions of lives and further strengthen the idea that microbes are responsible for the disease, not the demon.

It was followed by the great discovery of DNA, the chemical key to hereditary. The molecule of DNA was first identified in 1869 by a Swiss chemist called Johann Friedrich Miescher. He named it nuclein. In 1881 Albrecht identified nuclein as nucleic acid and provided its present chemical name, deoxyribonucleic acid (DNA). He also isolated the five nucleotide bases that are the building blocks of DNA and RNA: adenine (A), cytosine (C), guanine (G), thymine (T), and uracil (U). he received a Nobel Prize for his work in 1910. Later, DNA double helix structure was discovered by James Watson and Francis Crick in 1953, and in 1962 they were also awarded Nobel Prize for their groundbreaking discovery.

Edwin Hubble (1889-1953), changed the way we thought of the universe. He discovered the cosmos. His observations and discoveries led to a change in the understanding of the universe.

Albert Einstein (1879-1955) came to light. He was the most influential scientist of the 20th century. His theory of general relativity was published in 1917 which was one of his important contributions to the study of the physical world. Einstein received the Nobel Prize for his contribution to 'Theoretical Physics' in 1921. The Einstein refrigerator is an important invention by Albert Einstein. The equation $e=mc^2$, formulated by Einstein, played a central role in the development of nuclear weapons

The National Aeronautics and Space Administration (NASA) was developed in1958. They focused on human and robotic spaceflight programs. Their first project was Mercury, an experiment to study the survival of man in space. The second was Gemini, a spacecraft that was built for two astronauts for a human trip to the Moon by the end of the 1960s. Project Apollo was successful in the moon landing in 1969. They carried out five more successful lunar landing missions through 1972. After the Skylab and Apollo-Soyuz Test Projects of the mid-1970s, NASA's recommenced human spaceflight experiments in 1981, with the Space Shuttle program which resulted in the construction of an internal space station. NASA made tremendous progress exploring other planets, too, and continues its space research in different directions.

During the 20th century digital revolution occurred with the development of the mathematics required for computation and data storage based completely on a binary code. The second remarkable discovery revealed the information encoded in the molecular sequence of DNA. As per Francis Collins, DNA is the information molecule of all living things, as God's language, and the elegance and complexity of our bodies. It transmits the instructions from a cell and thus is the blueprint of life. The field of molecular biology emerged as the study of how genetic information is transmitted from one generation to another and is read out to form functional cellular components and regulatory circuits. Synthesis of the first complete gene, a yeast t-RNA, was demonstrated by Har Gobind Khorana and coworkers in 1972. He shared Nobel Prize for his work with other two coworkers. The foundational science of molecular biology subsequently led to the development of the biotechnology industry which dominated genome sequencing research for quite some time during 1980-90.

In recent years, NASA made tremendous progress in aeronautic research. NASA has also completed the investigation of the solar system, with the extreme study of all the planets. Using the Hubble Space Telescope, NASA has also dramatically changed our understanding of the universe, especially our planet. NASA's work on launch vehicles, communication satellites, and weather satellites has changed daily life and created whole new industries. Efforts are being made to find life on other planets. Since humans first began to wonder if there was life beyond Earth, one of the first places of hope to find was on Mars. NASA made five attempts and still hoping to find some traces of microorganisms down on the deep surface of Mars. Other countries such as China, India, and Russia are also in the race to find life on Mars and have sent their rockets over there. Recently, NASA developed the James Webb space telescope which is more powerful and sophisticated than the Hubble space telescope. Investigation of the galaxies through James Webb telescopes changed the old concepts of the universe. The expansion of the universe and the Big Bang theory are in question. Images taken verifies some galaxies are surprisingly small, sharp, and older than the Big Bang occurrence. That means the Big Bang theory is questionable. Nevertheless, the study of the galaxies through the James Webb telescope does not indicate any expansion of the universe.

Artificial intelligence is attributed to all these developments and enhancements in technology. There have been several artificial intelligence innovations that have created a great impact on human lives such as speech recognition, virtual assistants, chatbots, autonomous vehicle, face recognition, acute stroke care, cyber defense, and robots.

Given the above discussion and the progress made by modern technology in all walks of life even capturing the Moon and Mars, revealing secrets of the Milky Way galaxy including many more discoveries of the parallel universe, science is still lagging religion. With the evolution and civilization of humans, religions are also moving ahead. State-of-the-art temples, churches, mosques, and shrines are being constructed to worship their respective Gods and Goddesses. People all over the world have blind faith in their chosen religion and God. Nations are fighting by the name of their religions. With the advancement of technology, religions are also getting resilient. Believers in religion are becoming staunch in their blind faith day by day and are intolerant towards other religions, resulting in more unrest and chaos in the world. People are turning mad and defensive of their religion. Religion divides people, controls people, and eludes people. If people stay above the steadfast religion and believe in spirituality, then this chaos can be mitigated to a great extent in this world.

All the world's major religions should emphasize love, compassion, patience, tolerance, and forgiveness instead of criticizing each other religion. They should respect the person and his religion and allow him the freedom to follow any religion as per his or her liking and prejudices.

> "In the beginning, there was only darkness
> that stretched out to infinity".
> – *Rig Veda*

Chapter Three
Concept of God in Different Religions

"All religions are man-made; God has not yet revealed Himself beyond doubt to anybody."
— *Bangambiki Habyarimana, Pearls of Eternity*

The concept of *God* exists since antiquity. All religions worship this concept in one way or the other. Some worship millions of deities whereas some do none but worshipping the concept of God as superhuman power is very strong. It is very pertinent to know the concept and meaning of God in different major religions to investigate the existence of God.

The current population of the world is 7.9 billion as per the United Nations estimate illustrated by Worldometer. The forecast for the year 2023 is 8.031billion. The most populated countries in the world are China (1.41billion), India (1.38 billion), the United States (333 million), and Indonesia (272 million). Out of them, Christians are about 2.54 billion, Muslims are 1.92 billion, and Hindus are 1.07 billion.

The major world religions are Judaism, Christianity, Islam, and Hinduism. Around 1.1 billion people identify as agnostics, atheists, nonreligious, or secular *(Adherent.com)*. The meaning and concept of God in these major four religions are discussed in the present chapter.

There are about 4300 recognized religions in the world which comprise churches, temples, mosques, congregations, faith groups, tribe cultures, and movements.

The world's primary religions fall into two groups. First is Abraham's religion such as Christianity, Judaism, and Islam as illustrated in Figure 1. Abraham in about 2000BC was considered the spiritual father of these three monotheistic (One God) religions. He was the founder of Judaism and had a great influence on Christianity and Islam. He was born in Iraq. Abraham's religion is- God is one, eternal, omnipotent, omniscient, and the creator of the universe.

Before starting Judaism, he used to worship idols, particularly the moon which was considered the source of fertility for crops, herds, and families. Prayers and offerings were offered to the moon to invoke its blessing.

The second category is Indian religions which include Hinduism, Buddhism, Sikhism, Jainism, Brahma Kumaris, and some small groups.

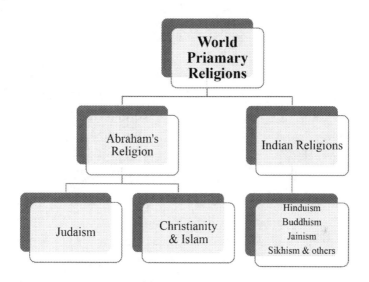

Figure 1: World Primary Religions

There is an *unaffiliated class* also which covers all those who profess no religion, from atheists, and agnostics to people with spiritual beliefs but no link to any established religion.

Among the 1.1billion *unaffiliated* people around the world, over 700 million people, or 62% of them in China where they make up 52.2% of the national population. Japan comes next with the second largest unaffiliated population in the world with 72 million or 57% of the national population. After that United States of America, 51 million people 16.14% of Americans said they have no link to an established faith.

India is a highly populated country has only 13% non-religious,

3% atheist, and 3% not sure about their commitment to any faith (Bhayana, 2015).

People who believe in God are called Theists and the faith is known as Theism. Theists believe God is beyond the universe, time, and space. He controls the universe. Another class is Deist and faith is Deism, a religious belief that God created the universe and established rationally comprehensible moral and natural laws but does not intervene in human affairs through miracles or supernatural revelation. Atheists do not believe in God. Agnostic, neither believe nor deny God.

Early religion started with Paganism which is *the ancestral religion of the whole of humanity.* This ancient religious outlook remains active throughout much of the world today, both in complex civilizations such as Japan and India and in less complex tribal societies worldwide. Pagans believe that the divine manifests in all creations. Divinity is a part of nature. The faith has the freedom to worship the God and Goddesses of an individual choice. It is a polytheistic nature-worshipping religion.

There is another section of people called Pantheists who believe in Pantheism. Pantheism is derived from Greek words, Pan meaning *all,* and Theos, meaning *God.* Pantheist believes, "I feel God is in everything." The belief that the Universe and Nature are divine. It fuses religion and science, and concerns for humans with concerns for nature. It provides the most realistic concept of life after death and the most solid basis for environmental ethics. It is a religion that requires no faith other than common sense, no revelation other than open eyes and a mind open to evidence, and no guru other than yourself. In other words, God is one, God is all. All is God, God is all.

Some are Naturalistic Pantheists, who see nature as God. Those who believe in nature and God, as one reality, are Spinoza. Spinoza's most famous and provoking idea is God is not the creator of the world, but that the world is a part of God. The concept was given by Baruch Spinoza (1632-1677) an Amsterdam philosopher. When Albert Einstein asked about his belief in God. He said, "I believe in Spinoza's God who reveals Himself in the lawful harmony of the world, not in a God who concerns Himself with fates and actions of human beings." Spinoza's God does no punishment since there is no judgment. His God does not believe in fate and Karma's theory. Spinoza completely rejected the idea of a personal God. God is not a being who judges or cares about what people eat and how they pray. He did not create the universe willingly but through the necessity of his nature. This is a denial of God who answers prayers or speaks in the form of scriptures. Spinoza denied miracles because everything in the world must follow the law of nature. Spinoza believed in a *substance*. An infinite perfect essence with an infinite number of attributes of which all things in the universe are only finite modes. To Spinoza this one *substance* that is the totality of all existence, the kind of essence of reality itself is God. "Whatever is, is in God, and nothing can be or be conceived without God.' He also conceded nature as God and articulated, "From the necessity of the divine nature there must follow infinitely many things in infinitely many modes."

There is another branch of Pantheism known as Panentheism. A doctrine that the universe exists within God, but that God nevertheless transcends or has some existence separate from the universe. God is the first material cause of the world. God is all in all. Lord Krishna also mentioned in Bhagwat Gita, "By Me, all this universe is pervaded through my unmanifested form. All beings abide in Me but I do not abide in them." Bhagwat Gita (Chapter ix- 4). That means all the universe in Me, but I am still aloof. I am like the air that runs into every living being and even touches the nonbeing but remains aloof.

Pandeism believes in a God who created the universe and then ceases to interfere in its operation, whereas panendeism proposes the universe had a creator and this creator used its substances as the material of the universe. After creation, He imparted all its substances into the universe and ceased to interfere or interact with the universe. Panendeism explains that any identity with the power and intelligence necessary to create a universe such as ours would have been able to carry out this creation correctly and do not need to interfere with the creation once it has been initiated.

The most important message we will ever realize is that we will always be a part of this invisible and unbroken thread of the Eternal Oneness of life (God): even when our minds are full of thoughts, beliefs, physical senses, and conditionings trying to tell us otherwise.

After the concept of a different kind of belief, it is pertinent to understand the definition and idea of God in various major world religions.

God in Judaism:

Judaism is the religion of Jews. Abraham was the first Jew, the founder of Judaism, and the physical and spiritual ancestor of the Jewish people, God is named *Yahweh*. The Judaic God is omnipotent, omniscient, and omnipresent. God revealed himself to Abraham, Moses, and the Hebrew prophets. The Judaic God exists outside of the universe rather than as a part of it. He is kind and upright. He is the creator of the universe. He is aware of the thoughts and feelings of every person. He is formless. Their holy books are *Torah*, the *Neviim*, *the Ketuvim,* and *the Talmud.* It is a monotheistic religion,

God in Christianity:

Bible represents the Christian religion which comprises the Old and New Testaments. The Old Testament runs parallel to the Jew's Torah and consists of the same material. New Testament illustrates the biography of Jesus Christ. Christian philosophy believes God exists outside the Universe and created everything. God is a trinity, the Father, the Son, and the Holy Spirit. The Holy Spirit, also known as Holy Ghost, is assumed as the intermediary between God and man and "The outpouring grace of God and the effulgent rays that emanate from His Manifestation." This concept is different from Judaism which states God is only one, formless and merciful judge. Christians believe God is benevolent, loves all people, all-knowing, all knowledgeable. Those who have faith in Christ will be rewarded with eternal life in heaven. They strongly consider Christ as their savior who sacrificed his life for their sins. Christian religion believes in preaching, promoting, and converting to Christianity.

God in Islam:

Quran is the holy book. Quran is the literal words of God as conveyed directly to their prophet Muhammad by God. God in Islam is called *Allah*. The religion is bifurcated from Abraham's religion and is 1400 years old. Islam also believes in one God who is outside the Universe. He is omniscient, omnipotent, and merciful. He demands and rewards obedience who follow Quran only while punishing wrongdoers. Islam rejects the divinity of Christ but believes assiduously in promoting and converting to Islam. Islam is actively engaged in proselytizing people from other religions.

God in Hinduism:

Hinduism is the third most prevalent and oldest religion in the world. It is over 5000 years old. Hinduism is not a religion; it is a lifestyle-a way of living. The religion of Hindus is *Sanatana Dharma*, meaning eternal balance or eternal way of living, absolute duties, and practices. The term *Sanatan* meaning which has no beginning or end. It is everlasting, timeless, non-sectarian, infinite, and unchangeable. *Dharma* means duty or religion. In other words, duties are performed according to one's spiritual identity as *atman* (Self) and are thus the same for everyone. General duties include virtues such as honesty, refraining from harming living beings, purity, benevolence, mercy, endurance, self-control, kindness, and austerity.

The concept of God in Hinduism is simple as well as complicated. It is a misconception that there are 330 million gods. The Sanskrit word for *ten million* also means *group*, and *330 million devas* originally meant 33 types of divine manifestation. Hindus do not worship or even know the names of all gods. It is an overall misinterpretation that it is a polytheistic religion. Hinduism believes in only one God but permits its followers to worship God in many forms such as nature, trees, the sun, idols, animals, and divine Avatars like Lord Krishna, Lord Rama, Lord Shiva, and Lord Vishnu. Furthermore, many goddesses such as Laxmi, Durga, Kali, and Saraswathi are also worshipped. They are not to be confused with the One and the Supreme God. God is a different thing than a deity or a god or goddess. These words should not be confused together. These divine beings are called devas (gods) and devis (goddesses). These are celestial beings that control the forces of nature. Hinduism can be identified as Pagan.

However, there is one concept of the trinity where Vishnu, Brahma, and Shiva are considered Gods. Brahma is the creator of the universe, Vishnu is the preservative and Shiva is the destroyer of the universe. In practice, Hindus do not worship 330 million gods, but they do worship many gods and goddesses as His manifestation. It is fascinating to note that many of these deity metaphors are similar to gods and goddesses that existed in pagan pantheons, ancient Greece, and Persia. Hindu religion also believes in reincarnation and Moksha. Soul's ability to merge with God and get rid of the cycle of birth and death. There are many Holy Scriptures such as four Vedas, 108 Upanishads, Maha Puranas (18), and Bhagwat Gita. Most Hindus follow the Bhagwat Gita which summarizes all of them. Hinduism does not proselytize like other religions.

God in Shinto:

It is the indigenous religious beliefs and practices of Japan. The word Shintō means, *the way of kami* a divine power, precisely the various gods or deities. The term was used to distinguish indigenous Japanese beliefs from Buddhism. Shintō has no founder, no prophet, no official sacred scriptures, and no fixed philosophy. Shinto gods, spirits, supernatural forces, and essences are known as *kami.* There are 120 Gods and Goddesses in Shintoism.

Ancient Shintō was polytheistic. People found *kami* in nature, which ruled seas or mountains, as well as in outstanding men. They also believed in *kami* of ideas such as growth, creation, and judgment. Though each clan made the tutelary *kami* the core of its unity, such *kami* were not necessarily the ancestral deities of the clan. Sometimes *kami* of nature and *kami* of ideas were regarded as their custodial *kami*. The main beliefs of Shinto are:

- Purity is physical cleanliness, avoidance of disruption, and spiritual purity.
- Physical well-being.
- Harmony exists in all things and must be maintained against imbalance.
- Procreation and fertility.
- Family and ancestral solidarity.
- Subordination of the individual to the group.
- Reverence to Nature.
- All things have the potential for both good and bad.

The soul (*Tama*) of the dead can influence the living before it joins with the collective *kami* of its ancestors.

Shinto shrines, or *jinja*, are the sacred locations of one or more *kami,* and there are some 80,000 Shinto shrines in Japan. Certain natural features and mountains may also be considered shrines.

God in Buddhism:

Buddhism is an Indian religion or philosophical tradition based on a series of original teachings ascribed to Gautama Buddha. It originated in ancient India as a Sramana tradition sometime between the 6th and 4th centuries BCE, spreading throughout Asia. It is the world's fourth-largest religion with 520 million followers. Buddhism comprises a variety of traditions, beliefs, and spiritual practices mostly based on the Siddhartha Buddha's teachings which are followed as

- The world is full of sorrows.
- Desire is the root cause of all sorrows.

- Sorrow can be conquered by conquering desire.
- Desire can be conquered by following the eight-fold paths: *Right understanding, Right Resolve, Right speech, Right action, Right living, Right efforts, Right thoughts, and Right concentration.*

Buddha did not believe in God or the soul. He emphasized more on *karma* and *ahimsa* (non-violence). He was against the Caste System. Buddha taught in *Pali. Pali* is the language used to preserve the Buddhist canon of the Theravada Buddhist tradition, which is regarded as the oldest complete collection of Buddhist texts surviving in an Indian language. *Pali* is closely related to Sanskrit, but its grammar and structure are simpler. Moreover, it was the common dialect of that time in and around the area of Buddha's native place.

His main teachings point to nonattachment, the concept of *me* and *I* is an illusion, desires are the cause of suffering and are content with the circumstances and reach Nirvana which is not a place, like heaven, but more a state of being in harmony with the universe.

God in Jainism:

Jainism is a religion derived from ancient India. It began to gain importance in India in the 6th century BC. There are about six million followers throughout the world. Jainism is a religion promulgated by a 'Jina'. Principles articulated by a 'Jina' constitute Jainism and the follower of Jainism is known as a 'Jaina'. Further, a 'Jina' is neither a supernatural being nor an incarnation of God. The word 'Jina' means the conqueror or the victorious, one who has conquered worldly passions with one's strenuous efforts. 'Jinas' are persons of this world who have attained supreme knowledge, subjugated their passions, and are free from any sort of attachment. Jainism is a set of principles preached by such persons known as 'Jinas'. Jainism is not a religion propounded by a non-human being or based on a sacred book of non-human origin. On the contrary, Jainism is a religion of purely human origin, and it has emanated from the mouth of a dignitary who has secured omniscience and self-control through efforts. Thus, the people who worship the Jina and who follow the religious tenets proclaimed by the Jina are called the Jainas and their religion is Jainism.

The most common element of Jainism is its belief in non-violence which also extends to the right speech, thoughts, and everyday life. Jainism also includes five life principles which include reincarnation, but it doesn't consider the idea of a creator, God.

The fundamental principles of Jainism can be briefly stated as follows.

The first fundamental principle of Jainism is man's personality is dual. It comprises material and spiritual. The Soul is bound by subtle particles of matter known as Karma. It considers that just as gold is found in an alloy form in the mines, in the same way, souls are found along with the Karma bondage from time eternal. The impurity of the soul is thus treated as an existing condition that needs to purify like gold from its crude form.

The second principle discloses that man is not perfect on account of the existence of Karma in the soul. To obtain perfection for the human soul in that true and eternal state, it should have four characteristics, *Infinite perception or faith, Infinite knowledge, Infinite Power, and Infinite bliss.*

The third principle states that though man is not perfect, he must control his material nature. It is only after the entire subjugation of matter that the soul attains perfection, freedom, and happiness. By the control of senses and thoughts man will be able to sail across the ocean of births and can achieve perfection.

The last principle reveals that it is only everyone that can separate his soul and the matter combined with it. The separation cannot be affected by any other person. This means that man alone is responsible for his good or bad actions in his life. He cannot excuse himself from the responsibility of experiencing the fruits of his actions.

No God, nor His prophet or deputy or beloved can interfere with human life. The soul, and that alone, is directly and necessarily responsible for all that it does. *God is regarded as completely unconcerned with the creation of the universe or with any happening in the universe. The universe goes on of its own accord.* Because of this definite attitude towards God, Jainism is accused of being atheistic. It is true in the sense that Jainism does not attribute the creation of the universe to God. But at the same time, Jainism cannot be labeled as atheistic because it believes in Godhood, numerable gods, merits and demerits, religious practices, etc. According to Jainism, the liberated soul is considered God and it is concerned with the task of creation of this world. This principle distinguishes Jainism from other religions, e. g., Christianity, Islam, and Hinduism

God in Sikhism:

In the early 21ˢᵗ century there were about 25 million Sikhs worldwide. The religion originated in the Punjab region of the Indian subcontinent. Its followers are known as Sikhs meaning "seeker" or "learners". There are ten Gurus in the Sikh religion. Upon the death of the 10ᵗʰ, Guru Gobind Singh (1666–1708), the spirit of the eternal Guru transferred itself to the Holy Scripture of Sikhism, *Guru Granth Sahib (The Granth as the Guru)*. The Sikh place of worship, or Gurdwara, is more than a place of worship. It has historically served as a refuge for the homeless and the destitute.

History and Philosophy of Sikhism:

Sikhism believes in a universal God, common to all mankind, not limited to any religion, nation, race, creed, color, or gender. The Sikh religion is strictly monotheistic, believing in one supreme Creator, free of gender, absolute, all-pervading, and eternal. Sikhism views life as a unique opportunity to discover and develop the divinity within each of us. Human rights and justice are the keystones of Sikh belief,

Sikhism was a movement within the Hindu tradition; Guru Nanak Dev Ji, was born and raised a Hindu and eventually belonged to the Sant tradition of northern India, a movement related to the great poet and mystic Sant Kabir (1440–1518). The Sants, most of whom were illiterate, composed hymns of great beauty articulating their experience of the divine. They believed that devotion to God is essential to liberation from the cycle of rebirth in which all human beings are trapped; unlike the followers of bhakti, however, the Sants maintained that God is *Nirgun* ("without form") and not *Sagun* ("with form"). For the Sants, God can be neither incarnated nor represented in concrete terms. Chief among them was the Nath tradition, which comprised a cluster of sects, all claiming descent from the semi-legendary teacher Gorakhnath. Some scholars have argued that the Sants were influenced by Islam through their contact with the Mughal rulers of India from the early 16th century, but there is little indication of this, though Sufism (Islamic mysticism) may have had a marginal effect.

The Ten Principles Beliefs of the Sikh Religion are

1. Sikhs believe in one creator and are against worshiping demi-gods or idols. "God" in Sikhism is regarded as an all-pervading spirit without gender or form, which is approached through dedicated meditation.
2. Treat everyone equally.
3. Live by three principles- be always absorbed in meditation and prayer, make an honest income by honorable methods, share earnings, and selflessly serve others.
4. Sikhs believe that egotism is the biggest hindrance to connecting with the timeless truth of God. Sikhs practice daily prayer and meditation to reduce the effects of ego and prevent indulgence in the manifestations of ego: avoid the five sins of ego- Pride, Lust, Greed, Anger, and Attachment
5. Become Baptized: For many Sikhs, a voluntary ritual baptism is a critical part of religious practice. It symbolized becoming spiritually reborn by taking part in the baptism ceremony conducted by the "Five Beloved" Sikhs, who prepare and administer immortalizing nectar (Amrit) to initiates.

6. Keep the code of Honor: Sikhs carefully live according to a specific individual and communal standards, both ethical and spiritual. They are encouraged to forsake worldly worries, abide by the guru's teachings, and practice daily worship.

7. Wear Five articles of faith: Sikhs wear five visual signs of their dedication to their faith:
   Wear the Sikh undergarment for modesty and health. Wear a wooden comb in the turban to keep hair clean and untangled. Wear a steel wristlet as a sign of faith. Wear hair uncut, to honor the creator's intention. Wear a small sword symbolic of defending the religious rights of all faiths.

8. Follow the four Commandments: Sikh's four commandments include prohibitions against four behaviors: *Do not dishonor the creator's intention by cutting the hair. Do not harm the body with tobacco or other intoxicants. Do not eat sacrificial meat. Do not commit adultery*

9. Recite the five daily Prayers

10. Take Part in Fellowship

Given the above discussion on various religions, it is evident that devotees are fiercely attached to their personal or impersonal God. They have blind faith in their chosen God or religion. In the majority of cases, starts from early childhood. Nobody is born believing in God. If one is born into a Christian family, he or she follows Christianity. Likewise, if born into a Muslim family, the child follows Islam. Similarly, a person born into a Hindu family, follows Sanatan Dharma, the religion of Hindus. A few examples are there, where people change their religion during their lifetime as per their likings and prejudices.

Religion is a faith or belief in certain philosophy. There are about 4300 active religions in the entire world. Their preaching is different, but their goals are the same. All religions preach good morals and ethics, if followed make a person a perfect human being. However, certain people consider their religion is the best and if one does not follow that religion, he or she is an infidel. It is not out of the way to quote here Wole Soyinka, who said," I cannot belong to a nation which permits such barbarities as stoning to death and amputation- I do not care what religion it is."

In view of the above, it is concluded that God is one and resides in all living beings. All religions merge into one God who has no religion except love. The holy scriptures of these religions reveal amazing information and depth of divinity. Prophets like Jesus, Muhammad, Buddha, Shankaracharya, Guru Nanak Dev, and many more guided the world in the right direction sanctified with morals and ethics. However, translation and interpretation of their preaching have been crucified by some of their staunch followers. One should follow any discipline or religion but not abuse or degrade other religions and rather respect them instead of fight, hating, and killing people by religion.

> "A man can no more diminish God's glory by refusing to worship Him than a lunatic can put out the sun by scribbling the word 'darkness' on the walls of his cell."
> — *C.S. Lewis, The Problem of Pain*

Chapter Four
Eminent Scientists: Believers in God

"The idea that excites me the most concerns the two greatest puzzles in science: the origin of the universe, and the origin of consciousness."

— *Michio Kaku*

B oth science and spirituality are pursuing truth. One is searching for the outer world whereas the other is searching for the inner world. Both have the same goal, but their ways and approaches are entirely different. Science is limited to the realm of objective observation. It relies on testable empirical evidence and observation. Religion relies on subjective belief in creation. It is beyond intellect and reasoning. All intellect and reasoning are part of existence. So, science is a part of consciousness. Without being conscious, scientists cannot think. Without consciousness, nothing can be known. How can we solve a problem when we are part of it? Moreover, scientists are not creators but discoverers.

The existence of God has intrigued philosophers and scientists for thousands of years. But can modern science ever hope to crack this mysterious phenomenon? The existence of God has been a challenging problem for scientists since ever its conception. It has been a riddle for scientists who could not solve the mystery until today. They desperately want to find concrete proof of this mystery. Many of them tried to explain it but their explanations were not comprehensive. On the list of long-ago scientists who believed in God are Galileo, Descartes, Pascal, and Newton; more modern names, such as Lord Kelvin, Max Planck, and Francis Collins. They could not deny the presence of an unknown intelligent power who created and runs the universe. Some of the examples are given below.

Galileo Gallie (1564-1642) was an Italian physicist, astronomer, and philosopher. He was known as the Father of Astronomy. Galileo's Telescope is an attribute to his name. He believed in God. As per

Galileo, "Laws of nature are written by the hand of God in the language of mathematics." He believed in the existence of God and said, "I do not feel obliged to believe that the same God who has endowed us with sense, reason, and intellect has intended us to forgo their use."

Rene Descartes (1596-1650) was a French philosopher, scientist, and mathematician. He had an interest in metaphysics and cosmology. He was called the Father of Modern Philosophy. Descartes believed in the existence of an omnipotent, benevolent, and veracious God. He further articulated, "I have concluded that the evident existence of God and that my existence depends entirely on God in all the moments of my life, that I do not think that the human spirit may know anything with greater evidence and certitude."

Isaac Newton (1642-1726) was an English mathematician, astronomer, and physicist who is widely known for his pioneer work in physics, Newton's Laws. The first Nobel Prizes were awarded in 1901, while Sir Isaac Newton died in 1727. He expressed his views about God, "I know not how I seem to others, but to myself I am but a small child wandering upon the vast shores of knowledge, every now and then finding a small bright pebble to content myself with while the vast ocean of undiscovered truth lay before me." Newton's conception of God permeated his entire scientific work: "God's universality and eternity express themselves in the dominion of the laws of nature. Time and space are regarded as the 'organs' of God. All is contained and moves in God but without having any effect on God himself."

Max Planck (1858-1947) a German Physicist, originator of quantum theory, and Nobel Laureate, articulated that the concept of God is important to both religion and science, but in different ways, "Both religion and science require a belief in God. For believers, God is in the beginning, and for physicists, He is at the end of all considerations. To the former, He is the foundation, to the latter, the crown of the edifice of every generalized worldview." He strongly believed in God.

Guglielmo Marconi (1874-1937) an Italian electrical engineer known for his pioneer work in long-distance radio transmission and who shared the 1909 Nobel Prize in Physics, said, "The more I work with the powers of Nature, the more I feel God's benevolence to man; the closer I am to the great truth that everything is dependent on the Eternal Creator and Sustainer; the more I feel that the so-called science I am occupied with, is nothing but an expression of the Supreme Will, which aims at bringing people closer to each other in order to help them better understand themselves."

Werner Karl Heisenberg (1901-1976) a German theoretical physicist and the Nobel Prize winner, said, "Belief in God is a natural result of studying science. The first gulp from the glass of natural sciences will turn you into an atheist, but at the bottom of the glass God is waiting for you." He was a religious man and believed "Religion is, therefore, the foundation of ethics, and ethics the presupposition of life."

Carl Sagan (1934-1996) an American astrophysicist stated, "Science is not only compatible with spirituality; it is a profound source of spirituality. When we recognize our place in an immensity of light-years and the passage of ages, when we grasp the intricacy, beauty, and subtlety of life, then that soaring feeling, that sense of elation and humility combined, is surely spiritual. The notion that science and spirituality are somehow mutually exclusive does a disservice to both." He strongly believed in God, religion, and spirituality. "The cosmos is within us. We are made of star-stuff. We are a way for the universe to know itself"

Brian Josephson and William Daniel Phillips, great physicists and Noble Laureates, also believed that the universe was created through the action of intelligent power. William said, "I believe in God because of a personal faith, a faith that is consistent with what I know about science."

Nobel Prize winners Erwin Schrödinger and Wolfgang Pauli also held the belief that the universe was created by an intelligent power. Erwin was the most famous scientist who believed in God. Although he was raised in a religious Lutheran family. However, he had a strong interest in Eastern religions and pantheism, and he used religious symbolism in his works. He also believed his scientific work was an approach to Divinity. He was more inclined to Indian Vedanta philosophy. He believed, "Vedanta teaches that consciousness is singular, all happenings are played out in one Universal consciousness and there is no multiplicity of selves. In a famous essay on determinism and free will, he expressed very clearly the sense that consciousness is a unity, arguing that this insight is not new...From the early great Upanishads, the recognition Atman = Brahman (the personal self-equals the omnipresent, all-comprehending eternal self) was in Indian thought considered, far from being blasphemous, to represent, the quintessence of deepest insight into the happenings of the world."

Arno Penzias (b1933) a Nobel laureate, believed that the universe was the result of a supernatural plan. He expressed, "If there are a bunch of fruit trees, one can say that whoever created these fruit trees wanted some apples. In other words, by looking at the order in the world, we can infer purpose and from the purpose, we begin to get some knowledge of the Creator, the Planner of all this. This is, then, how I look at God. I look at God through the works of God's hands and from those works imply intentions. From these intentions, I receive an impression of the Almighty."

Charles Townes (1915-2015) another Nobel Laureate, assumed the existence of God since science could not explain the origin of the universe. Thus, he believed there was a need for some religious or metaphysical explanation. He believed in the concept of God and His existence. He said, "I feel the presence of God. I feel it in my own life as a spirit that is somehow with me all the time." He said that his scientific idea including those that led to the invention of the laser and maser came to him in spiritual life epiphanies. He also said that the religious, spiritual, and scientific discoveries were much alike in many ways since each required faith, a method of inquiry and observation, and unproven assumptions.

Richard Smalley (1943-2005) a Nobel Laureate, believed the fine-tuning of the universe was designed and created by God. He stated, "God did create the universe about 13.8 billion years ago, and of necessity has involved Himself with His creation ever since. The purpose of this universe is something that only God knows for sure, but it is increasingly clear to modern science that the universe was exquisitely fine-tuned to enable human life. We are somehow critically involved in His purpose. Our job is to sense that purpose as best we can, love one another, and help Him get that job done."

George David Wald (1906-1997) an American scientist and Nobel Laureate in medicine, believed "Consciousness was not produced by matter and that matter and life existed only because of preexisting consciousness. Mind, rather than being a late development in the evolution of organisms, had existed always; this is a life-breeding universe because the constant presence of the mind made it so. What we recognize as the material universe, the universe of space and time and elementary particles and energies, is then an avatar, the materialization of primal mind."

Arthur Compton (1892-1962) an American physicist and a Nobel Laureate, believed that the "orderly unfolding of the universe demonstrated a plan created by God. It is not difficult for me to have this faith, for it is incontrovertible that where there is a plan there is intelligence - an orderly, unfolding universe testifies to the truth of the most majestic statement ever uttered - In the beginning, God."

Nikola Tesla (1856–1943) a Serbian-American inventor, electrical engineer, and physicist, best known for his contributions to the design of the modern alternating current (AC) electricity supply system, not only believed in God but also followed Indian Vedanta like Erwin Schroder. Tesla said, "My brain is only a receiver. In the universe, there is a core from which we obtain knowledge, strength, and inspiration. I have not penetrated the secrets of the core, but I know that it exists."

Albert Einstein (1879-1955) a famous German American Scientist and Nobel Laureate said, "Natural laws were designed by intelligence, everyone who is seriously involved in the pursuit of science becomes convinced that a Spirit is manifested in the laws of the universe – a Spirit vastly superior to that of man, and one in the face of which we with our modest powers must feel humble.

In this way, the pursuit of science leads to a religious feeling of a special sort, which is indeed quite different from the religiosity of someone more naive." Einstein believed the problem of God was the "most difficult in the world." He said the question that could not be answered by a simple yes or no" and "the problem involved is too vast for our limited minds." Einstein did not believe in a personal or anthropomorphic God, considering that type of conception naive. He believed in a pantheistic God, He further articulated that "A human being is a part of the whole, called by us, "Universe," a part limited in time and space. He experiences himself, his thoughts, and his feelings as something separated from the rest — a kind of optical delusion of his consciousness. This delusion is a kind of prison for us, restricting us to our desires and affection for a few persons nearest to us. Our task must be to free ourselves from the prison by widening our circle of compassion to embrace all living creatures and the whole of nature in its beauty."

Antony Hewish (1924-2021) a British inventor and Nobel Laureate in physics, said, "I believe in God. It makes no sense to me to assume that the Universe and our existence is just a cosmic accident, that life emerged due to random physical processes in an environment which simply happened to have the right properties."

Kurt Gödel (1906-1978) an Austrian American Logician, mathematician, and philosopher, did not believe in materialism, or that the mind was produced by the brain, or that the brain evolved through Darwinian evolution. A brain is a computing machine connected with a spirit. He believed a human was a spirit connected with a physical body and that there were beings higher than humans and other worlds than earth. The world in which we live is not the only one in which we shall live or have lived. There are other worlds and rational beings of a different and higher kind.

It is not out of the way to mention Guru Nanak Dev (1469- 1539) a renowned Indian mystic and first Guru of the Sikh, cited in his version of *Japji Sahib* that there were 18,000 worlds in this universe and some superpower runs the universe. It is amazing, how he could imagine the unmanifested universe at that time.

Michio Kaku (b1947) A highly respected American theoretical physicist and futurist known for his pioneer work on string theory said, "I have concluded that we are in a world made by rules created by an intelligence. Believe me, everything that we call chance today won't make sense anymore. To me, it is clear that we exist in a plan which is governed by rules that were created, shaped by a universe intelligence, and not by chance."

Francis Collins (b1950) One of the most respected physician-geneticists in the world, astonished the world when he became a Christian after his interactions with patients who were dying. As a scientist, he has undoubtedly stated that he once thought that the origins of the universe and all its processes could be explained with mathematical equations. Now, he believed in the existence of God. He stated, "As a believer, I see DNA, the information molecule of all living things, as God's language, and the elegance and complexity of our bodies and the rest of nature as a reflection of God's plan. I had to admit that the science I loved so much was powerless to answer questions such as *what is the meaning of life? Why am I here? Why does mathematics work, anyway? If the universe had a beginning, who created it? Why are the physical constants in the universe so finely tuned to allow the possibility of complex life forms? Why do humans have a moral sense? What happens after we die?"* He further added, "I have found there is a wonderful harmony in the complementary truths of science and faith. The God of the Bible is also the God of the genome. God can be found in the cathedral or the laboratory. By investigating God's majestic and awesome creation, science can be a means of worship."

David Russel Humphreys (b1942) is an American young earth creationist. He has proposed a theory for the origin of the universe which allegedly resolves the distant starlight problem that exists in young earth creationism. According to him, Bible provides a foundation for cosmological thinking and teaches cosmological egocentricity. After finding God, he stated that it was God who made the planets with spinning automatic nuclei, thus explaining their orientation.

Emil Silvestru (b1954) is a Romanian geologist and an expert in karst sedimentology including caves. After becoming a Christian, he quickly realized that the 'millions of years' interpretation, so common in geology, was not compatible with Genesis. "Once I became a Christian,' Emil says, 'I knew I had to "tune-up" my scientific knowledge with the Scriptures. Although philosophically and ethically I accepted a literal Genesis from my conversion, at first, I was unable to match it with my technical side." He also believed that scientific facts interfered with his beliefs and adjusted both facts and beliefs to make them compatible with each other.

Sarah Salviander (b1979) is an astrophysicist who studies extreme deep-space phenomena, mostly quasars, supermassive black holes, and giant galaxies. She grew up in a non-religious family. She believes in God and eventually became a Christian. Sarah now works in astrophysics research at the University of Texas. Sarah's studies in cosmology led her to be "astounded and blown away, completely and utterly awed" by the order of the universe. During a lonely year, while she was in a different state from her husband and all her family, Sarah read a book, *The Science of God* by Gerald Schroeder. "I was intrigued by the title, but something else compelled me to read it. Maybe it was the loneliness, and I was longing for a deeper connection with God." Sarah was very impressed by Schroeder's book: "It proved to me that Genesis 1 was scientifically sound, and not just a "silly myth" as atheists believed. I realized that, remarkably, the Bible and science agree." Sarah Salviander realized that the universe was trying to communicate to her that God existed, and after some time doubting the message, she accepted it as God in her life.

There are numerous examples of famous scientists who could not deny the presence of some supernatural power balancing and running the universe. Some atheists think that modern science has removed the need for God. However, many of the greatest scientists believe just the opposite, they strongly feel the existence of an intelligent designer of the universe, a kind of supernatural power.

Very recently, scientists claim that quantum theory proves consciousness moves to another universe at death. A book entitled, *Biocentrism: How Life and Consciousness are the Keys to Understanding the True Nature of the Universe,* has baffled scientists. It reveals that life does not end when the body dies, and it can last forever. The author of the book *Robert Lanza* is an eminent scientist and physician who believes in this theory of biocentrism which means life and consciousness are fundamental to the universe. Consciousness creates the material universe, not material creates the consciousness.

A recent investigation by Stuart Hameroff and British physicist Roger Penrose revealed that consciousness resides in the microtubules of the brain cells, which are the primary sites of quantum processing. Upon death, this information is released from the body. They are coming closer to the Hindu Vedanta concept about the soul leaves the body after death.

A survey taken in 2009 records that 33 percent of scientists believe in God and another 18 percent in a higher power, compared to 94 percent of the general public. That means 51percent of scientists, believe in the existence of God.

"The existence of God is not subjective. He either exists or does not. It is not a matter of opinion. You can have your own opinions. But you can't have your own facts."
—*Ricky Gravis*

Chapter Five
Eminent Scientists:
Nonbelievers in God

*"Science adjusts its views based on what's observed. Faith is
the denial of observation so that belief can be preserved."*
                                              — *Tim Minchin*

ew hundred years ago, atheism was in minority. Atheists were
not recognized and respected at that time. However, with the
passage of time conditions changed. Atheism is generating
quite a lot of attention these days. Presently, atheism is widely
accepted but still religion is pulling many strings and dominates the
entire globe. Scientists always argued about the existence of God
since they were looking for some evidence. Due to a lack of evidence,
some of them were not comfortable accepting the existence of God.
However, these people had been very successful in their profession
by discovering new concepts beneficial to mankind. In other words,
they were genius. It is very pertinent to know their views about the
existence of God. Some of the famous scientists who did not believe
in the existence of God are given below:

Linus Pauling (1901-1994) a chemist, author, and peace activist
won the Nobel Prize in Chemistry in 1954. In 1962, he earned a
Nobel Peace Prize as a peace activist, thus making him the only
person in history to have two unshared Nobel prizes. While he was
initially a Christian, he became an atheist later in his life. About God,
his thoughts were "I am not, however, militant in my atheism. The
great English theoretical physicist Paul Dirac is a militant atheist.
I suppose he is interested in arguing about the existence of God. I
am not. It was once quipped that there is no God and Dirac is his
prophet."

Marie Curie (1867-1936) was one of the pioneers of radioactivity
research, she was the first woman to win two Nobel Prizes for
Physics and Chemistry. She was also the first woman professor at

the University of Sorbonne. She was a Catholic, but her mother and sister's death changed her to agnosticism.

Peter Higgs (b 1929) Founder of the Higgs Boson particle, or the *God particle* as it came to be popularly known. Peter Higgs, won the Nobel Prize in Physics in 2013 for his work and has been particularly annoyed by the name "God particle." He is an atheist. God particle has nothing to do with religion. He is 92-year-old.

Jean-Paul Sartre (1905-1980) was a famous atheist, creative novelist, philosopher, and playwright. He won the Nobel Prize for Literature in 1964 but refused to accept the award, stating that it was against his beliefs to accept awards for his work. His views about God, "If God did not exist, everything would be permitted and that, for existentialism, is the starting point. Everything is indeed permitted if God does not exist, and man is in consequence forlorn, for he cannot find anything to depend upon either within or outside himself. He discovers forthwith that he is without excuse."

Paul Dirac (1902-1984) He was a well-known physicist and was acclaimed as the founder of quantum physics. He shared Nobel Prize in Physics in 1933. He was a candid atheist and criticized religion strongly. According to him, "The very idea of God is the product of human imagination."

Francis Crick (1916-2004) A biologist, biophysicist, and neuroscientist, he was one of the founders of the DNA molecule, a discovery that got him the Nobel Prize in Physiology or Medicine in 1962. Crick was against organized religions and was a strong atheist. His view about God is, "God is a hacker, not an engineer."

Francois Jacob (1920-2013) was born to a Jewish family and raised with the religion, he did not believe in it and soon after his bar mitzvah, he announced that he was an atheist. He discovered the effect of *E Coli* on enzymes and was awarded the Nobel Prize in Medicine in 1965.

Hermann Joseph Muller (1890 -1967) was an American geneticist, and Nobel laureate best known for his work on the physiological and genetic effects of radiation. He earned a Nobel

Prize in 1946 for Physiology or Medicine. He belonged to a catholic religious family but remained an atheist throughout his life.

Pierre Curie (1859-1906) was a French physicist who was the husband of Marie Curie, Pierre and Marie won the Nobel Prize in physics for their research on radiation. Pierre did not believe in religion.

Stephen Hawking (1942-2018) an English theoretical physicist, and cosmologist, mentioned in his famous book,

The Grand Design is that quantum theory is the theory of everything. There is no soul, no consciousness, and no free will. Human beings are biochemical robots governed by the brain. Many conventional physicists and scientists follow the same belief. One of them, Francis Crick (1916-2004), co-discoverer of DNA, said that awareness is nothing more than a feeling generated in the brain and "You, your joys and sorrows, your memories and your ambitions, your sense of personal identity and free will, are no more than the behavior of a vast assembly of nerve cells and their associated molecules."

Stephen Hawking further elaborated his view by saying, "It is hard to imagine how free will can operate if our behavior is determined by physical law, so it seems that we are no more than biological machines and that free will is just an illusion." It is astonishing to know the views of these intellectuals about their denial of the soul, free will, or consciousness. They did not know that their intellect and denial both prevail in the consciousness. If the brain is running the entire process, then who is running the brain? The brain is like a computer unable to function without electricity. That electricity is absolute consciousness. Hawkins's views about God: "I am an atheist." "God may exist, but science can explain the universe without the need for a creator." "I believe the simplest explanation is, there is no God. No one created the universe, and no one directs our fate.

Jacques Lucien Monod (1910-1976) was a French biologist who contributed greatly to the understanding of the Lac operon as a regulator of gene transcription in cells, suggested the existence of mRNA molecules in the process of protein synthesis, and further contributed to the field of enzymology. He was awarded the Nobel

Prize in Physiology or Medicine in 1965. Monod wrote the book *Chance and Necessity* in 1970, which became a popular primer on the relationship between the roles of random chance and adaptation in biological evolution and provided much ammunition to the atheist community by proposing that the natural sciences revealed an entirely purposeless world that undermines the traditional claims of the world's religions. His views also contributed to the development of the idea of "Memes" that Richard Dawkins, a famous atheist made famous in his writings.

Richard Feynman (1918-88) was an American theoretical physicist. He was an atheist and nonbeliever in Abraham's anthropomorphic Gods. About the existence of God, he said, "Is there God? How sure can we be there is a God."

Subrahmanyam Chandrasekhar (1910-1995) has a space-based X-ray observatory named after him, launched by the space shuttle Columbia on July 23, 1999. He was an Indian-American astrophysicist, best known for his work on the theoretical structure and evolution of stars. Awarded the Nobel Prize in Physics in 1983 for his important contributions to knowledge about the evolution of stars. He was the author of many books and recipient of many awards. He was associated with famous scientists Paul Dirac and Niels Bohr. The *Chandrasekhar limit,* which is the maximum mass of a stable white dwarf star, is named after him. In an interview with Kevin Krisciunas at the University of Chicago, on 6 October 1987, Chandrasekhar commented: "Of course, I was an atheist."

James Dewey Watson (b. 1928) received the Nobel Prize in physiology or medicine in 1962 as a co-discoverer along with Francis Crick and Maurice Wilkins of the molecular structure of DNA. When asked by a student if he believed in God, Watson answered, "Oh, no. Absolutely not. The biggest advantage to believing in God is you don't have to understand anything, no physics, and no biology. I wanted to understand."

Steven Weinberg (b 1933) is an American physicist best known for his work on the unification of electromagnetism and the weak force, for which he shared the Nobel Prize in physics in 1979 His popular science books and articles combine explaining science in the added context of history, philosophy of science, and *atheism*. In a 1999 speech in Washington, D.C., he said, "With or without religion, good people can behave well, and bad people can do evil, but for good people to do evil – that takes religion."

David Takayoshi Suzuki (b 1936) is a Canadian zoologist, geneticist, science broadcaster, and environmental activist. His work in television began in 1970 with the weekly children's series, Suzuki on Science, going on to host CBC's The Nature of Things and the acclaimed PBS series A Planet for the Taking. He also worked in radio, hosting CBC Radio One's Quirks and Quarks, and a weekly program for more mature audiences called Science Magazine.

Though he has been often accused by his critics of turning his environmental causes into a religion of its own, Suzuki describes himself in his autobiography as an atheist with no illusions about life and death.

Leonard Susskind (b1940) is an American physicist specializing in string theory and quantum field theory. He is Felix Bloch professor of theoretical physics at Stanford. He is a notable promoter of public understanding of science, and his entire course on quantum physics can be downloaded on the iTunes platform from Stanford. His contributions to theoretical physics are voluminous, including the independent discovery of string theory, the theory of quark confinement, the development of Hamiltonian lattice gauge theory, the holography principle, the string theory of black hole entropy, and the principle of "black hole complementarity." Susskind is also a popular speaker for both science and against religious creationism. In a review of the book, The Cosmic Landscape: String Theory and the Illusion of Intelligent Design, Michael Duff wrote that Susskind is "a card-carrying atheist."

Stephen Jay Gould (1941-2002) was a paleontologist, evolutionary biologist, and historian of science who became one of the most influential popularizers of evolutionary biology through his books and essays. Though a critic of the deterministic view of human behavior and society, he contributed much to expanding upon the mechanisms of natural evolution. He generated some controversy with A Scientific Dissent from Darwinism, taking issue with the gradualism and reductionism of orthodox Neo-Darwinists. He contributed "Punctuated Equilibrium" to the evolutionary lexicon to explain the fossil evidence of abrupt changes in organismic form interspersed with long periods of stability. Himself an atheist, Gould was an advocate for what he called "Nonoverlapping Magisteria" (NOMA) as a way to resolve the conflicts between science and religion. "Science and religion occupy two separate realms of human experience," he wrote in *Rock of Ages.* "Demanding that they be combined detracts from the glory of each."

Richard Dawkins (b 1941) is the most prominent scientific atheist in the world today and was the Charles Simonyi Professor of the Public Understanding of Science at Oxford until his retirement in 2008. Dawkins' particular brilliance is not so much reflected in radical discoveries in his field of biology, but in his popular science writings like his books *The Selfish Gene and The Extended Phenotype.* He has been called "Darwin's Rottweiler" in the press for his strong support of evolution by natural selection. He has also written against creationism in the book *The Blind Watchmaker* and against theism in *A Devil's Chaplain* and *The God Delusion*, both popular best-sellers. An engaging and energetic speaker, Dawkins promotes atheism as senior editor and columnist for the Council for Secular Humanism's Free Inquiry magazine, and as a member of the editorial board of Skeptic magazine since it was founded. In 2006 Dawkins founded the Richard Dawkins Foundation for Reason and Science, and in 2007 founded the atheist "Out" campaign, and in 2008 he supported the Atheist Bus Campaign, Britain's first atheist advertising blitz.

David Sloan Wilson (b1949) is Suny Distinguished Professor of Biology and Anthropology at Binghamton University in New York. Dr. Wilson, who describes himself as a "nice atheist" views religions as a sort of mega-trait that evolved because it conferred advantages on believers. He explored this theme in his book, *Darwin's Cathedral: Evolution, Religion and the Nature of* Society. Not a supporter of Richard Dawkins' public efforts to organize atheists, Wilson described atheism as a "Stealth Religion" on the political blog Huffington Post in 2007.

Paul Zachary Myers (b1957) known as "PZ," is an evolutionary developmental biologist and professor of biology at the University of Minnesota, Morris. He is an energetic promoter of science generally and evolution in particular. He got involved in the use of the internet for this purpose and was a founding member of the pro-evolution website The Panda's Thumb, and created his web blog, Pharyngula, in 2002. PZ Myers has become the leader of the science-focused online atheist movement and his brilliance as an atheist might be said to be the remarkable success he has had in this position. Pharyngula received the Koufax Award in 2005 for 'Best Expert Blog', and Nature named it the top-ranking blog written by a scientist. His increasing popularity as a proponent of atheism has him a popular speaker at free thought, atheist, and humanist events.

Given the above, it is concluded that Atheists wanted proof of the existence of God. God exists beyond time and space where we exist in time and space. So, God's existence cannot be proved.

"I have noticed even people who claim everything is predestined, and that we can do nothing to change it. Look before they cross the road."
—Stephen Hawking

Chapter Six
Celebrities: Nonbelievers in God

"Beliefs don't change facts. Facts, if you're reasonable, should change your belief."

— *Ricky Gervais*

Today about 2.3 percent of the world's population identifies themselves as an atheist, and nearly 12 percent or more describe themselves as nontheist – non-believers in any deity. Atheists are present in all walks of life and throughout history as well. They have been very successful in their professional life. It is also very relevant to know their views about God. The most prominent and recognized atheists of all time are described as follows:

Andrew Carnegie (1835-1919) was a famous American industrialist, businessman, and philanthropist. A Scottish-born immigrant, he established the Carnegie Steel Company in Pittsburgh and later merged it with the Federal Steel Company to become U.S. Steel. He is regarded as the second richest man in history, then he gave most of his steel and railroad fortune away to establish libraries, schools, and universities all over America. He wrote many books on wealth and its responsibilities, on social issues, and on political philosophy. He self-identified as a positivist and kept away from organized religion. Carnegie preferred naturalism and science, saying in his autobiography, "Not only had I got rid of the theology and the supernatural, but I had found the truth of evolution."

Sigmund Freud (1856-1939) was an Austrian psychiatrist who founded the psychoanalytic school of psychology. Using his theories of the unconscious mind and defense mechanisms of repression, his psychoanalysis sought to cure sufferers of psychopathology through a dialogue between the patient and his psychoanalyst. He had an elaborate system for the interpretation of dreams as indicators of unconscious desire. His philosophical writings established his strong advocacy for a worldwide view, and he was eulogized as "the atheist's touchstone" for the 20th century. His expression about God was, "The idea of God was not a lie but a device of the unconscious which needed to be decoded by psychology. A personal God was nothing more than an exalted father figure: desire for such a deity sprang from infantile yearning for a powerful, protective father, for justice and fairness, and for life to go on forever. God is simply a projection of these desires, feared and worshipped by human beings out of an abiding sense of helplessness. Religion belonged to the infancy of the human race: it had been a necessary stage in the transition from childhood to maturity. It promoted ethical values essential to society. Now that humanity had come of age, however, it should be left behind."

Clarence Seward Darrow (1857-1938) was an American lawyer and a recognized defense attorney. His most famous case was the defense of Tennessee teacher John Scopes in the "Monkey Trial" against the state law that barred the teaching of evolution. The prosecution side was argued by William Jennings Bryan, and the trial served as the story for the play and later film, Inherit the Wind. During the trial, Darrow self-identified as an agnostic by saying, "I do not consider it an insult, but rather a compliment to be called an agnostic. I do not pretend to know where many ignorant men are sure – that is all that agnosticism means." His writings like *Absurdities of the Bible* and *The Myth of the Soul* emphasized that his agnosticism was strong enough to be atheism.

George Denis Patrick Carlin (1937-2008) was one of the most popular and controversial comedians during his lifetime, having won five Grammy awards for his comedy albums. He was the very first guest host for Saturday Night Live and is considered one of the most brilliant satirists of American culture. He was most noted for his focus on psychology, religion, the English language, and any other subject that might shock and delight his audiences. He came in second on the Comedy Central network's list of 100 Greatest Comedians of all time. An outspoken atheist, Carlin joked in his book *Brain Droppings* that he worshipped the sun because he could see it. He also introduced in an HBO special the *Two Commandments*, a condensed version of the ten ending with one additional commandment, *Thou Shalt* keep thy religion to thyself.

Bruce Jun Fan Lee (1940-1973) was an American-born Chinese martial artist, philosopher, instructor, and actor, the founder of the Jeet Kune Do combat form. When he turned to the development of his martial arts form in the 1960s, he also became notable for his views and practices of promoting peak physical fitness with proper training, diet, and vitamin supplements. Bodybuilder Arnold Schwarzenegger was influenced by Lee and described his physique as defined, with very little body fat. "I mean, he probably had one of the lowest body fat counts of any athlete. And I think that's why he looked so unbelievable." Lee had majored in philosophy at the University of Washington and kept an extensive library of philosophy. His first book expressed a well-developed philosophical outlook and was entitled *Chinese Gung-Fu: The Philosophical Art of Self-Defense.* As he developed Jeet Kune Do, he cited influence from Taoism, Jiddu Krishnamurti, and Buddhism but was himself an atheist who expressed disbelief in God.

Katherine Houghton Hepburn (1907-2003) was a celebrated actress in film, television, and stage for 73 years. She received four Academy awards for best actress in a film. In 1999, the American Film Institute ranked Hepburn as cinema history's greatest female star. She married socialite businessman Ludlow Ogden Smith in 1928 but divorced six years later. Despite several romances, the love of her life was Spencer Tracy, with whom she made nine movies. When asked about her faith in God in one of the interviews, she said that while she agreed with Christian principles and thought highly of Jesus Christ, she had no personal religious beliefs nor any belief in an afterlife. "I am an atheist and that's it. I believe there's nothing we can know except that we should be kind to each other and do what we can for other people."

Warren Edward Buffett (b1930) is an American businessman and CEO of Berkshire Hathaway rated by Forbes as the richest person in the world (in the first half of 2008, before the Wall Street meltdown). He is noted for adherence to the philosophy of "value investing" and for accepting an annual salary for himself of less than $200,000. Compare that to what taxpayers are now paying the CEOs of failed Wall Street investment firms! Buffett is further noted for his philanthropy, a passion he shares with fellow billionaire Bill Gates, along with a weekly bridge play date. In 2006 Buffett announced that 83% of his fortune would be going to the Bill and Melinda Gates Foundation for further philanthropy. He describes himself as religiously agnostic. In Roger Lowenstein's 1995 biography Buffett: The Making of an American Capitalist, he is described as non-religious. "He adopted his father's ethical underpinnings, but not his belief in an unseen divinity."

John Rogers Searle (b1932) is an American philosopher whose contributions to the philosophy of mind, philosophy of language, and social philosophy made him an influential member and spokesperson for the Free Speech Movement in Berkeley during the late 1960s and early '70s. Drawing upon his theory of intentionality, Searle argued in his book *The Rediscovery of the Mind* that much of modern philosophy has attempted to deny the existence of consciousness, with little success among conscious people. The primary issue Searle identifies is a philosophical false dichotomy between strong materialism and subjective, first-person experience of the world. What emerged from his resolution is a view he calls "biological naturalism" – that consciousness is real, caused by the physical processes of the brain. Searle is regarded as an atheist who believes in freedom of will and has argued eloquently (and controversially) for that position.

Stephen Gary "Woz" Wozniak (b1950) is a computer engineer who founded the Apple computer company with Steve Jobs. The two became friends while working on a mainframe during the summer of 1970. The two sold some possessions to raise $1,300 and assembled the prototypes in Job's garage. They formed the company on April 1, 1976, and priced their Apple I personal computer at $666.66.

Wozniak is a committed philanthropist, funding various educational projects. Since leaving Apple he founded other ventures to produce things like the first universal remote and wireless GPS.

He's a member of the Silicon Valley Aftershocks Segway polo team, which won the 2008 Woz Challenge Cup. Woz calls himself "atheist or agnostic," in that he says he doesn't know the difference between the designations.

David John Chalmers (b1966) is an Australian philosopher, director of the Center for Consciousness, and past director of the Center for Consciousness Studies at the University of Arizona in the U.S. His book *The Conscious Mind* is considered a seminal work on consciousness and its relation to issues in the philosophy of mind, even by its physicalist detractors. Chalmers argues for an essentially dualistic view of the mind which he terms, "naturalistic dualism." Chalmers sits on the editorial board of the Journal of Consciousness Studies and his paper published there characterizing the mind-body problem in terms of philosophical zombies generated more than twenty response papers from such notables as Daniel Dennett, Francisco Varela, Francis Crick, and Roger Penrose, and the exchanges are still among the most valuable literature debating the philosophy of consciousness ever generated. As an atheist, says Chalmers, "The simulation hypothesis has made me take the existence of a god more seriously than I ever had before".

Sean M. Carroll (b1966) is a theoretical cosmologist specializing in general relativity and dark energy. Currently, he is a Senior Research Associate in Physics at Caltech, writes scientific books and textbooks in his areas of expertise, contributes to the blog Cosmic Variance, writes articles for science magazines such as Nature, and is a popular presenter and lecturer at scientific symposia. Carroll is perhaps better known for his strong advocacy of atheism. He argues that scientific thinking must lead to a materialistic worldview and a rejection of all notions of a deity or spiritual nature. Carrol believes, almost all Cosmologists are Atheists.

Karl Marx (1818-1883) Karl Marx was a German philosopher and economist, but he's widely acclaimed as the world's most prominent socialist thinker. His social theories have influenced many socialist revolutions around the world and triggered the rise of communism and modern socialism. Even his philosophy has been named in his honor as Marxism. His opinion on religion can be found in many of his works, and one of his best-known expressions is, "Religion is the sigh of the oppressed creature, the heart of a heartless world, and the soul of soulless conditions. It is the opium of the people."

George Bernard Shaw (1856-1950) was one of the most well-known and prominent scriptwriters in history. His unbelievable and thought-provoking plays earned him the Nobel Prize for Literature in 1925. His thoughts on God were, "I am an atheist and I thank God for it." About religion, he said, "There is only one religion though there are a hundred versions of it."

Ernest Hemingway (1899-1961) was a novelist who earned the Nobel Prize for Literature in 1954. He was raised in a religious family and went to church regularly in childhood. However, he was against organized religion. His feelings towards God were, "I do not like to write like God. It is only because you never do it, though, that the critics think you can't do it." About religion, he said, "Creation's probably overrated. After all, God made the world in six days and rested on the seventh."

Bertrand Russell (1872-1970) was one of the most prominent philosophers and mathematicians. He was awarded the Nobel Prize for Literature in 1950. He did not believe in the existence of a god or gods, and he was an antagonist of organized religion.

Pablo Neruda (1904-1973) was a Chilean poet, whose implausible works earned him the Nobel Prize for Literature in 1971. He was an atheist and did not like mystical religion.

Mikhail Gorbachev (1931-1991) was the last ruler of the Soviet Union. His policies of reform and openness resulted in the end of the Cold War with the US, though it also inadvertently led to the collapse of the Soviet Union. However, the world acknowledged his attempts to stop the war and awarded him the Nobel Peace Prize in 1990. Gorbachev was a *cultural atheist*. His views about God, "Nature is my God."

Wole Soyinka (b1934) is one of the most famous playwrights and poets currently alive and was the first African to win the Nobel Prize for Literature, in 1986. He is a peace-loving person. He said, "I cannot belong to a nation which permits such barbarities as stoning to death and amputation- I do not care what religion it is."

Though Soyinka grew up in a Catholic background, yet he is now an atheist and is critical of organized religion, especially Islam considering the brutality being carried out in the name of the religion. He said that he would be happy if there was no religion in the world.

Besides these celebrities, there are famous stars from Hollywood who do not believe in God. They are –Alan Cumming, Bill Maher, Billy Joel, Brad Pit, David Cross, Juliann Moore, Joaquin Phoenix, Jodie Foster, Howard Stern, Hugh Laurie, Ian McKellen, Kathy Griffin, Kevin Bacon, Morgan Freeman, Ricky Gervais, Stephen Fry, Uma Thurman, Woody Allen, and many more. It is difficult to cover all. Surprisingly, it is not out of the way to mention here that Morgan Freeman, the actor who played God in *Bruce Almighty* does not believe that God exists. According to Washington Post. Freeman said that God was just a 'Human Invention'.

> "The fact that a believer is happier than a skeptic is no more to the point than the fact that a drunken man is happier than a sober one".
> — *George Bernard Shaw*

Chapter Seven
Concept of Heaven and Hell

"I sent my Soul through the Invisible. Some letter of that
After-life to spell: And by and by my Soul returned to me and
answered: I myself am Heaven and Hell."
                    —Omar Khayyam (a Persian poet)

S everal religions of the world believe that the afterlife soul goes to *heaven* or *hell*. The term *Heaven* referred to the sky where the heavenly bodies exist. It is considered the dwelling of God and His angels and also the place where virtuous souls arrive afterlife. Heaven is usually interpreted as a spirit world of eternal bliss where spirits can acquire all the comforts of the universe. It is portrayed as a beautiful place with a clean environment and soft scented breeze flowing through the gorgeous gardens comprising elegant flowers of different colors and varieties. Other features of heaven are, scenic waterfalls and snowy mountains, dazzling colorful birds and butterflies, flying all over the place. Stunning animals run in the green meadows. Beautiful angels walking here and there. Sumptuous food served in golden cutlery by beautiful women in a splendid dining hall with golden furniture and sparkling chandeliers. A place of glory and enjoyment devoid of suffering, pains, and tears. In gist, heaven is considered a symbolic representation of luxury.

Likewise, *Hell* is an afterlife of suffering where the wicked or sinful souls are punished. Hell is almost represented as underground dungeons occupied by demons and surrounded by fire. It is portrayed as frightening, and an atrocious place with poisonous and dangerous animals.

Punishments in Hell are given by demons to sinful souls according to their sins. Awful sinners get severe punishments. However, the concept of heaven and hell in certain religions varies. It was thought desirable to take a bird's-eye view of the descriptions of heaven and hell in various religions to analyze the existence of Heaven and Hell.

Heaven and Hell in Christianity:

There are over two billion Christians in the world, the vast majority of whom believe in heaven and hell. According to them, both places are the eternal dwelling place for the soul. After life, the soul goes either to everlasting bliss or torment. Since Jesus died for the sins of humanity and took their punishment to himself so that no human being would ever end up in Hell. Thus, there is a very little description of hell in the New Testament. Moreover, Jesus did not believe in the concept of hell. As per Christianity, *Heaven* is the place of glory and eternal bliss devoid of pain and suffering. It is shared by all the virtuous and chosen.

Heaven and Hell in Hinduism:

There are about 1.2 billion Hindus all over the world, majority of them are in India. The concept of Heaven and Hell in Hinduism is slightly different from that of other religions due to their faith in reincarnation. Hinduism is based upon two fundamental laws. The law of Karma and the law of transmigration. Souls go to heaven and hell as per their good or bad actions. The soul transmigrates from one life to another until it purifies itself. Here the stay of the soul is temporary, until the next birth. The permanent stay of the soul in heaven is possible by attaining Moksha. Moksha is the liberation of the soul from the cycles of birth and death. As per Hinduism, the entry of the soul into heaven and hell is decided based on good and bad actions (Karma) and is not limited by religion. Virtuous people with good karma go to Heaven to enjoy the fruit of their good actions whereas wicked people with sinful actions (Karma) are sent to Hell to undergo the punishments for their bad deeds. These punishments comprise dipping the souls in boiling oil, burning them in fire, and torturing them with various weapons and poisonous snakes. Souls who complete their punishments are reborn in rich or poor families as per their actions (karma). They will continue the cycle of birth and death until they purify themselves by their good deeds. Present and past karma of each birth are taken into account for future birth.

Seven Heavens in Hinduism:

As per the Puranas, one of the holy scriptures of Hinduism, there are seven higher worlds of the heavens and seven lower worlds. All worlds are meant for humans' afterlife. Upon death, the god of death, Yama, accounts for a person's life and determines how long they will stay in the higher and lower worlds as per their Karma earned during their most recent incarnation. When the requisite stays have been accomplished, the soul is reincarnated again on earth.

The seven heavens of Hinduism are as follows:

Satyaloka: the abode of Brahma. Most virtuous sages live here.
Tapaloka: the place of the second-greatest sages.
Janaloka: the world for the life-long celibates.
Maharloka: the place for those who voluntarily went through a period of celibacy.
Svarloka: a group of planets that are home to lesser deities, bards, and other pious beings
Bhuvarloka: the atmosphere of the earth; home to ghosts and spirits caught in limbo before their rebirth.
Bhurloka: the earth and other planets with similar attributes; the only place people can accumulate good or bad karma

The seven lower worlds are known as Patal Loka (the world under the earth) believed to be ruled by demons and snakes. The 7 Patalas are *Atalaloka, Vitalaloka, Sutalaloka, Talatalaloka, Mahatalaloka, Rasatalaloka and Patalaloka.*

Different realms of Patala are also called Nag-Loka. These are ruled by different demons and Nagas (snakes in human form): Vayu Purana (scripture) records each realm of Patala has cities in it. The Vishnu Purana (scripture) describes a visit by the divine nomadic sage Naroda Muni to Patala. Narada illustrates Patala as more beautiful than Heaven. It is comprised of splendid jewels, pleasant groves, marvelous lakes, and attractive demon maidens. The pleasing fragrance in the air is fused with soothing music. The soil here is white, black, purple, sandy, yellow, stony, and gold. The Bhagavata Purana (Holy Scripture) calls the seven lower regions Bila-svargas meaning *subterranean heavens.*

Below the regions of Patala lies *Naraka*, the Hell – the realm of death where sinners are punished. The sinful soul undergoes punishment in the lower worlds according to the severity of their sins.

A soul could spend time in both, heaven and hell — for instance, if a lifelong celibate did some evils they needed to work off. If enough good karma is earned, the soul can finally break out of the cycle of birth and death and reach Nirvana.

Heaven and Hell in Buddhism:

Buddhism religion is also widely spread throughout the world with over 500 million followers. The Buddha explained the existence of other worlds, of heavens and hells populated by celestial beings.

As per the Buddhist texts, there are thirty-one planes of existence in the universe, comprising humans. Beings are born into a particular plane depending on the types of their accumulated actions (Karma).

Below the human plane is four planes (*Asura, Peta, Thiracchana, and Niraya*) which are designated as unhappy states of existence. Beings are born into these states as a result of their sinful karma. Excessive greed and attachment to worldly belongings may cause re-birth in the *Peta* plane and be drawn to the place of attachment.

Heaven:

Above the human plane are the Deva and Brahma planes. As the level of the plane becomes higher, more subtle is the state of existence and longer is the life span in that plane.

The devas have physical forms which are more subtle than that in the human plane. They also possess supernatural powers. Brahma planes are illustrated as form and formless states (*rupa* and *loka*). The Brahmas in the form state (*rupa loka*) have material forms even more subtle than that of Devas. They have only three sense faculties; sight, hearing, and the mind. In the formless states (*arupa loka*), the beings are devoid of any material bodies. They transcend all physical sensations and exist in a state of tranquility. In general, the beings in the higher planes are invisible to the beings in the lower planes of existence. Humans cannot see Devas or Brahmas unless they have attained special powers called *abhinna,* through the practice of special meditation. Beings in these higher planes are designated as celestial beings and their life span last billions of years relative to earthly life. Though the lifespans in these higher planes of existence last longer, but they eventually come to an end. The existence in all these planes is conditioned and depends upon the laws of cause and effect.

Hell:

There are many beliefs about Hell in Buddhism. Several hells are described as places of great suffering for those who commit evil actions, such as cold Hells and hot Hells. Like all the different realms within cyclic existence, an existence in Hell is temporary for its inhabitants. Those with sufficiently negative karma are reborn there, where they stay until their specific negative karma has been exhausted, at which point they are reborn in another realm, such as that of humans, hungry ghosts, animals, and of demons, all according to the individual's karma.

Heaven and Hell in Judaism:

There are about 15.2 million Jews in the world. 45.3 % are living in Israel. Most of them believe in Heaven and Hell.

As per the Jewish religion, there are seven *heavens*. Allotment of these heavens depends upon the good deeds of the individual soul. The most virtuous souls are near to God in the seventh *Heaven*.

1. **Shamayim**: The first Heaven, ruled by Archangel Gabriel, is the closest of heavenly realms to the Earth; it is also considered the dwelling of Adam and Eve.
2. **Raquia**: The second Heaven is dually governed by Zachariel and Raphael.
3. **Shehaqim**: The third Heaven, under the leadership of Anahel, serves as the home of the Garden of Eden and the Tree of Life.
4. **Machonon**: The fourth Heaven is ruled by the Archangel Michael,
5. **Machon**: The fifth Heaven is under the administration of Samael.
6. **Zebul:** The sixth Heaven falls under the jurisdiction of Zachiel.
7. **Araboth**: The seventh Heaven, ruled by Cassiel, is the holiest of the seven Heavens. It houses the Throne of Glory attended by the Seven Archangels and serves as the realm in which God dwells.

Hell:

Judaism used the word Gehenna for Hell. Gehenna is not Hell, but rather a sort of Purgatory where one is judged based on his or her life's deeds. The word Gehenna means a valley of Hinnom, the south wall of the city of Jerusalem where people tossed their trash and it used to burn all the time. So, it was a comparison with hell.

People are not in Gehenna forever; the longest that one can be there is said to be 11 months. Some consider it a spiritual forge where the soul is purified for its eventual ascent to Olam Habah (Heaven). When one has so deviated from the will of God, one is said to be in Gehenna. This is not meant to refer to some point in the future, but to the very present moment. The gates of teshuva (return) are said to be always open, so one can align his will with that of God at any moment. Being out of alignment with God's will is itself a punishment according to the Holly Torah.

Heaven in Islam:

Islam is the second largest religion in the world with about 2.0 billion followers. It is amazing that the religion is 1400 years old only and has a large following. The concept of heaven and hell in Islam is similar to that of Judaism and Christianity. Muslims believe on Judgment Day when Allah (God) decides based on individual deeds where to send the soul in, Jannah (Heaven) or Hell (Jahannam). The righteous will enter Jannah and the sinful in Jahannam. As per *Holy Quran: "Is the description of Paradise, which the righteous are promised, wherein are rivers of water unaltered, rivers of milk the taste of which never changes, rivers of wine delicious to those who drink, and rivers of purified honey, in which they will have all [kinds of] fruits and forgiveness from their Lord" (Quran, 47:15).*

Hell in Islam:

Muslims believe in Jahannam which derives from the Hebrew word Gehenna. Those who are wrongdoers and disbelievers will go to Hell or Jahannam.

Hell is the place for sinners after death on Judgment Day. In Holy Quran, the word "Jahannam" and "Al-Near" is mentioned the most. Muslims are obligated to pray five times a day and ask forgiveness and protection from hellfire in each prayer from Allah Almighty.

In the Qur'an, there are literal portrayals of the destined in a fiery Hell, as compared to the garden-like Paradise (Jannah) enjoyed by righteous believers. However, Satan is not viewed as Hell's ruler, merely one of its sufferers. The gate of Hell is guarded by Maalik also known as Zabaaniyah. The Quran states that the fuel of Hellfire is rocks/stones (idols) and human beings. Names of Hell according to Islamic Tradition are based on the Quranic ayah and Hadith.

Although generally Hell is often portrayed as a hot steaming and tormenting place for sinners there is one Hell pit that is characterized differently from the other Hell in Islamic tradition. Zamhareer is seen as the coldest and the most freezing Hell of all, yet its coldness is not seen as a pleasure or a relief to the sinners who committed crimes against God. The state of the Hell of *Zamharee*r is suffering from the extreme coldness of blizzards ice and snow which no one on this earth can bear. The lowest pit of all existing Hells is the *Hawiyah* which is meant for the hypocrites and two-faced people who claimed to believe in Allah and His messenger by the tongue but denounced both in their hearts. Hypocrisy is the most dangerous sin of all even though Shirk (setting partners with God) is the greatest sin viewed by Allah. In any case, there is good reason to believe that punishment in Hell is not meant to last eternally but instead serves as a basis for spiritual rectification.

Heaven and Hell in Sikhism:

There are about 25 million Sikhs in the world. The Sikh religion is born from Hinduism. So, some of the followers still believe in Hinduism. Most Sikhs as per their religion do not believe in heaven or hell. The main purpose of life, according to Sikhism, is to become one with God. This is pursued by a life focused on remembering the Creator always, earning an honest living as a householder, and sharing one's abundance with the destitute.

Heaven and Hell in Jainism:

The population of Jains is about five million. Most of them reside in India. Some of the largest Jain communities are present in Canada, Europe, Kenya, the US, Hong Kong, and Fiji. Like other religions,

Jainism also believes in the afterlife, reincarnation, and the doctrine of Karma. As per this law, every action, thought, or word produces an effect which in turn serves as the cause of another action and so on. This chain of cause and effect is known as Karmic Bondage.

To break the cycles of birth, death, and rebirth, one has to accumulate good deeds. Good deeds lead to Heaven, a place of eternal bliss and rest. There is no creation and recreation, no business, no hate, and rivalry. The righteous sit enthroned, their crowns on their heads, and enjoy the luster of the Divine Splendor. Permanent bliss is obtained by Moksha (salvation), meaning by getting rid of the cycle of birth, death, and rebirth. Attaining Moksha requires the annihilation of all good or bad Karma, if Karma are left it must bear fruits.

According to Jainism, hell is one of the four *gatis* (realms of existence) within which a soul transmigrates until it gets liberated from the cycle of birth and death. A soul reincarnates in one of the four *gatis* (form) as per its karma. Bad actions or karma result in the soul getting reincarnated in hell. The four *gatis* are: deva (demi-gods), manuṣya (humans), nāraki (hell beings), and tiryañca (animals, plants and micro-organisms).

Souls in hell determine their life span according to their karma. After suffering its life span in hell and bearing the consequences of its karma, a soul is reborn either as a human or in animal form.

To sum up the descriptions of heaven and hell of various religions, the following arguments arise.

The first fundamental question that comes to the mind, is there any proof of the existence of real heaven and hell described in these Holy Scriptures? A survey of literature does not show any proof of their existence. These descriptions are just fantasies. Metaphors of Heaven and Hell are imaginary since no one has visited these places during his or her lifetime. If someone has seen or imagined, it may be under the influence of psychedelics. There are some illustrations found where people have explained having near-death experiences. Many books are written on Near Death Experiences (NED). The most common occurrence is, seeing the white light or passing through a long tunnel and then going into paradise followed by an enchanting description of the paradise with all the beauty and luxury. This can be due to their hallucinations in the subconscious mind. Secondly, near death, a Christian sees Jesus Christ, a Hindu sees Krishna or Rama or Shiva his worship deity where a Muslim sees his Prophets, a Buddhist sees Buddha, Jain sees Bhagwan Mahavira and a Sikh sees one of his ten Gurus whom he worships. Why don't they see something different? Hindus should see Jesus Christ. Similarly, Christians and Muslims should see the Hindu deities. You see only whom you believe in or worship all the time since your childhood. Whatever is in the subconscious mind that is the near-death experience? The mind is a universe and can make a heaven of hell, a hell of heaven. Heaven and Hell are all in the mind.

Now the question arises, why do these religions illustrate heaven and Hell? It is very simple. Religions are manmade organized disciplines. To keep the community under discipline, they teach morals, ethics, and good deeds. There has to be some kind of fear to refrain people from bad actions and evils. There comes heaven and hell. If you have bad Karma, you will go to hell. With righteous actions, you will be rewarded in heaven. These are socially controlled devices to either encourage people to pursue virtues or petrify them from crimes.

Moreover, the soul is devoid of the physical body. If the soul undergoes any pleasure or suffering in heaven or hell respectively, it won't feel anything. You can't eat gourmet food or drink delicious wine, can't live in beautiful palaces, and even can't touch those 72 beautiful virgins in heaven. They remain virgins forever. It is just like a dream. During the dreams, there are still feelings. When you wake up, you have the sensations of that good or bad dreams. Good dreams give you pleasant feelings and bad one tears in your eyes. Since your body is linked with your soul, yes! you can have these emotions. In the other scenario, you do not have a body, or any identity so there won't be any feelings of pain or pleasure.

During reincarnation, the soul transmigrates to another body. There is no sign of the previous births. There are some books on reincarnations where people have revealed their previous births. These people also forgot their previous birth with time. Brian Weiss has described in his book *Many Lives, Many Masters* about the previous births. It is hard to believe those interviews of previous births described under the influence of hypnosis by the patients. One person revealed many previous births. How can a person keep those memories of the last births in his mind? Moreover, what is the proof of his narration of previous births? Amazing, it appears like fantasies. Though the book is quite famous and also got good reviews from well-known psychiatrists, still it is hard to believe the description of previous births.

There are many programs about Past Life Regression. People are undergoing this journey. Past life regression is a therapeutic technique that is used to analyze memories from one's past lives through hypnosis. Past lifetime regression has been practiced as a tool for uncovering latent issues of those who are not able to access their memory consciously. These psychotherapists believe that memories of past lives are stored in the brain. When a person experiences a trauma, the brain may be triggered to release these memories. This technique can help to identify details about the individual he was, the circumstance of his past life, key events, and places where energy or emotions have been blocked or stuck. Some kinds of latent fears may come to the surface which can be the cause of his anxiety and stress or related diseases.

This theory of past life regression has been analyzed and demystified by modern science but could not find any concrete evidence in favor of this therapy.

A religious person can have blind faith in these fantasies, but a spiritual person wants to analyze them by his or her own experiences. On the other hand, scientists need some concrete proof for the existence of Heaven and Hell and unfortunately could not find even one. So, it is concluded that heaven and hell are here on earth. People who are of good moral character, healthy, honest, hardworking, following the morals and ethics of life, and doing good deeds are in heaven. Those who are opposite of these characteristics are certainly in hell. What goes around comes around. What you sow, so shall you reap. To every action, there is an equal and opposite reaction. To every cause, there is an effect. Your richness won't take you to heaven unless you are rich with good deeds. As they say, "It is easier for a camel to pass through the eye of a needle than it is for a rich man to enter the kingdom of God."

The Vedas and Vedanta do not mention hell. The Puranas only illustrate the place of torture as hell. From the transcendental viewpoint, there is neither heaven nor hell. It is all mental creation. Very well-articulated by Persian poet Omar Khayyam, "I sent my Soul through the Invisible. Some letter of that After-life to spell: And by and by my Soul returned to me and answered: *I myself am Heaven and Hell.*" Heaven and Hell are within, the way you think. As they say, nothing is good or bad, thinking makes it so. Jesus Christ said, "The kingdom of God is within you." Vedanta also tells the same thing. *Eternal bliss is within*. Perennial joy is in your innermost self. Abandon the idea of heaven. The idea of obtaining eternal happiness in heaven is a futile dream and infantile idea. Seek the eternal bliss within. You are the immortal soul, a pure consciousness, ever blessed, ever free, all beyond time, space, and causation.

Thus, we need to focus on our present. Our past is what we are today, and our future depends upon our present. Who has seen Heaven or Hell, the afterlife? None. There is no proof of their existence. One can only see them after leaving this planet. There is no way that he can come back and tell his observations. So, both heaven and hell lie in your mind. It all arises from the mind. The only difference between heaven and hell is believing a thought. As heaven is your good memories and hell is your bad memories. Whether you want to enter heaven or hell. It's not in someone else hands. It's your own choice. Love is heaven and fear is hell. The real heaven is to live with righteous people who believe in love, honesty, and sincerity; the real hell is to live with wicked people who believe in money, power, wine, and women. Every choice one makes in his life brings him closer to the place he will go afterlife, Heaven or Hell.

Moreover, Heaven and Hell are not geographical, they are

psychological. Very well-articulated by an Indian mystic and philosopher Osho, "Hell and Heaven are within you, both gates are within you. When you are behaving unconsciously there is the gate of hell; when you become alert and conscious, there is the gate of heaven."

"Physicists abandoned their belief in a Newtonian material universe because they had come to realize that the universe is not made of matter suspended in empty space but energy."
—*Bruce H. Lipton*

Chapter Eight
Is there Life after Death?

*"The soul can never be cut to pieces by any weapon, nor burned
by fire, nor moistened by water, nor withered by the wind." It
is immortal.*

— Bhagavad Gita

T
he quest to know life beyond death has always been a most
fascinating one since time immemorial. The question of life
after death has remained an enigma through the ages. It is a
very intriguing and mysterious question everybody wants to know its
answer. However, it is beyond the comprehension of human knowledge
to explain this riddle. Nevertheless, the human mind would not accept
any mystic answer without any reasonable conclusion. The demand
of the time is for concrete evidence, not of solitary prodigies. All
religions and spiritual traditions have their concepts. There have been
many theories on this subject. Some of them are based on religious
principles, whereas others are on philosophical ones.

Most religions believe in *heaven* and *hell*. Souls travel to heaven
or hell after the death of the body and are awarded heaven or hell
according to their good and bad deeds respectively. There is a
detailed description of heaven and hell, too. However, the question
arises, who has seen heaven and hell? Is there any proof? The
concept of heaven and hell was introduced by some religions to
create fear in the minds of people to refrain from crimes. Swami
Sivananda a Hindu spiritual teacher, described the journey of the
soul after death in his book, *What Becomes of the Soul After Death.*
A very interesting journey is described comprising the soul traveling
through the ether, air, smoke, mist, cloud, and moon. Again, is
there any proof of this journey? The description of the journey of
the soul appears to be like fantasies. Most scientists have rejected
such claims for lack of scientific data. Science relies principally on
documentable facts and replicable evidence. Survival of the human

consciousness after the death of the body is a very complex and unknown phenomenon. Most information was collected based on near-death experiences (NDE) and reincarnation evidence. Most of them were on individual experiences. It is not easy to collect replicable proof.

Scientists have explored the biology behind 'out-of-body' experiences. They wanted to find out exactly what happens in the brain and the consciousness after the clinical death of the body.

When the heart stops beating no blood gets to your brain, and after about 10 seconds brain activity ceases. That is normally the official death point. Yet around 10% or 20% of people who are brought back to life from that point, which may be a few minutes or over an hour, report having consciousness. They all report being able to see what is happening. The scientists want to confirm whether these are real experiences or hallucinations, by cross-checking what the patients report that they saw happening from above, with the doctors and nurses who were present. They even revealed the conversations between the doctors and nurses. So far, hundreds of cases have been confirmed as accurate, to the astonishment of the medical staff.

If the rest of the study continues in the same direction, it will confirm that *consciousness continues even when the brain is not functioning.* In other words, consciousness is something separate from the physical brain and body.

Christof Koch, the Chief Scientific Officer of the Allen Institute of Brain Science, the Lois and Victor Troendle Professor of Cognitive and Behavioral Biology at California Institute of Technology, argued that the soul dies, and everything is lost when human beings lose consciousness. "You lose everything. The world does not exist anymore for you. Your friends don't exist anymore. You don't exist. Everything is lost."

Bruce Greyson, a Professor of Psychiatry at the University of Virginia, challenged Koch's view of consciousness. He said, "If you take these near-death experiences at face value, then they suggest that the mind or the consciousness seems to function without the physical body."

The latest research shows that consciousness survives after physical organs stop functioning. Studies prove the mind does not die with the body. "Scientists at the University of Southampton have spent four years examining more than 2,000 people who suffered cardiac arrests at 15 hospitals in the UK, US, and Austria. They found that nearly 40 percent of people who survived, described some kind of 'awareness' when they were clinically dead before their hearts were restarted."

Sam Parnia, Director of Resuscitation Research at Stony Brook University, School of Medicine and one of the world's leading experts on the scientific study of death, says, "We're pushing through the boundaries of science here, working against assumptions and perceptions that have been fixed. A lot of people hold this idea that when you die, you die; that's it. Death is a moment — you know you're either dead or alive. All these things are not scientifically valid, but they are social perceptions. New science is needed to explore this mystery."

A multi-disciplinary team was led by Sam Parnia to investigate an objective look at what happens to the mind/consciousness during and after death. Their findings revealed as follows: "The evidence thus far suggests that in the first few minutes after death, consciousness is not annihilated. Whether it fades away afterward, we do not know, but right after death, consciousness is not lost. We know the brain can't function when the heart has stopped beating. But in this case, *conscious awareness appears to have continued for up to three minutes into the period when the heart wasn't beating,* even though the brain typically shuts down within 20-30 seconds after the heart has stopped. This is significant since it has often been assumed that experiences about death are likely hallucinations or illusions, occurring either before the heart stops or after the heart has been successfully restarted, but not an experience corresponding with 'real' events when the heart isn't beating. Furthermore, the detailed recollections of visual awareness, in this case, were consistent with verified events." Sam and his team want to pursue their study from a scientific and medical perspective rather than approaching it from a religious or philosophical point of view. He has described in his book, *Erasing Death, The Science that is rewriting the Boundaries between Life and Death,* that there is a continuation of consciousness after physical death and modern science can reverse the phenomenon of death.

Most findings are based on near-death experiences which have not only little scientific plea but are also subjective and impossible to quantify. The scientists admit that they still don't know what is going on with human consciousness after death, even though the studies give concrete evidence that the consciousness can survive at least the first few minutes of bodily death and maintain sufficient awareness to observe the clinically dead body and its surroundings while awaiting resuscitation.

Very recently, scientists claim that quantum theory proves, consciousness moves to another universe at death. A book entitled, *Biocentrism: How Life Consciousness is the Keys to Understanding the Nature of the Universe* has perplexed scientists. It reveals that life does not end when the body dies, and it can last forever. The author of the book Robert Lanza is an eminent scientist who believes in this theory of biocentrism which means life and consciousness are fundamental to the universe. Consciousness creates the material universe, not the material universe creates the consciousness. The research is a scientific clue that consciousness survives clinical death, and while not all that conclusive, the study certainly opens the door for an expanding understanding of the relationship between the body and the soul. Man possesses within himself infinite possibilities. The unlimited source of power and wisdom is within him. He must unfold the divinity within.

The Soul will continue to exist after death. Before this birth, an individual has passed through countless lives. Lord Krishna says in the Bhagavad Gita: - "O Arjuna, both you and I have had many births before this; only I know them all, while you do not. Birth is inevitably followed by death and death by rebirth. As a man casting off worn-out garments taketh new ones, so the dweller in the body, casting off worn-out bodies, entered others that are new."

The Upanishad text of Hindu philosophy also proclaims, "Just as a caterpillar which has come to the top of a blade of grass, draws itself over to a new blade, so also does the soul draw itself over to a new body, after it has put aside its old body." Just as a goldsmith, having taken a piece of gold, makes another form, new and more beautiful, so also, verily the Atman or soul having cast off this body and having put away ignorance, makes another new and more beautiful form (Brihadaranyaka Upanishad).

Stephen Hawley Martin, a professional editor, and celebrated author, also strongly believed that consciousness survived death and that life force came to the physical dimension for a reason. He described in his book entitled, *The Science of Life after Death*, many examples of eminent scientists who believed that life exists after death. Ample information available in the book on Near Death Experience also indicates human consciousness lives on. The science of reincarnation along with the cosmology of soul evolution is also illustrated in the book.

Raymond Moody, the award-winning author of a very popular book, *Life after Life*, also tried to emphasize that consciousness is metaphysical and survives death. Raymond Moody continues to draw enormous public interest and generates controversy with groundbreaking work on the near-death experience and what happens when we die.

Robert Monroe, vice president of NBC Radio after leaving NBC, became famous for his research into altered states of consciousness. His book, *Journey Out of the Body* is very popular and emphasizes human consciousness lives on. The book coined the term out of body experience (OBE). In fact, the term 'out of body experience' was first introduced in 1943 by George Tyrrell, a famous English parapsychologist, in his book, *Apparitions*. Later, the term was adopted by other researchers.

Professor Carl Jung, an eminent scientist, and philosopher suffered clinical death in 1944. He had cardiac arrest, and no blood was passing to the brain. Doctors revived him by injecting adrenaline into his heart muscle, which started beating again. He described his out-of-body experience (OBE) in his book, *Memories, Dreams, and Reflections.* Jung recalls his delightful experience, "It seems to me that I was high up in the space. Far below, I saw the globe of the earth bathed in gloriously blue light. I saw the deep blue sea and the continents. Far below my feet lay Ceylon, and the distance ahead of me was the subcontinent of India. My field of vision did not include the whole earth, but its global shape was distinguishable, and its outlines shone with a silvery gleam through that wonderful blue light. In many places, the globe seemed colored or spotted dark green like oxidized silver. Far away to the left lay a broad expanse of the reddish-yellow desert of Arabia. It was though the silver of the earth had there assumed a reddish-gold hue. Then came the Red Sea, and far, far back—as if in the upper left of the map—I could just make out a bit of the Mediterranean. My gaze was directed chiefly towards that. Everything else appeared indistinct. I could also see the snow-covered Himalayas, but in that direction, it was foggy or cloudy. I did not look to the right at all. I knew that I was on the point of departing from the earth. Later, I discovered how high in space one would have to be to have so extensive a view – approximately a thousand miles. The sight from the earth from this height was the most glorious thing I had ever seen."

Stephen Braude, an American philosopher, parapsychologist, Editor in Chief of the *Journal of Scientific Exploration*, and Professor of Philosophy at the University of Maryland, believed that life existed beyond death. His book, *Immortal Remains: The Evidence for Life after Death*, is quite interesting and reveals some facts for demonstrating how life continues after death.

Eben Alexander, a famous neurosurgeon who performed over 100 brain surgeries, described his own experience in his book, *Proof of Heaven* that consciousness survived death. He contracted bacterial meningitis in the year 2008. The deadly infection paralyzed his brain and sent him into a coma. His entire neocortex, the outer surface of the brain, the part that makes us human was entirely shut down. His attending doctors gave him only a 5 percent chance of his survival. He came out of the coma after a week and revived his consciousness within 36 hours and was able to read his illness charts. He was reborn. He narrated his near-death experience, "During my seven days of coma, I not only remained fully conscious but also journeyed to a stunning world of beauty and peace and unconditional love…I underwent the most staggering experience of my life, my consciousness traveling to another level." He further explained, "Our spirit is not dependent on the brain or body. It is eternal and no one has one sentence worth of hard evidence that it isn't."

However, his colleagues were not convinced by his experience. For years, Eben Alexander had never been accepted for his near-death experiences. He was, after all, a neurosurgeon with sophisticated training and a good reputation. But his severe brain infection and recovery transformed his life completely.

Science can reveal information about the matter, but it is helpless as far as the world of consciousness is concerned. Science has been denying the presence of consciousness in the past but now struggling to investigate it by developing sophisticated techniques to study the brain, through neuroscience. However, it failed to understand how the material brain produces the immaterial sense of consciousness or true awareness.

Osho an Indian thinker, controversial mystic, and spiritual teacher, stated, "All that can be experienced is not necessarily explainable, and all that can be explained is not necessarily experienceable. Mathematics can be explained easily, but there is no corresponding experience. Science can be explained easily, but even the greatest scientist is not transformed by his knowledge."

During the end of the 19th century, physicists had been working with Newton's laws of motion. They were satisfied while applying these laws to their further research. However, these laws do not make sense while studying motion at the subatomic level. This gave birth to a new physics called Quantum Physics. There have been many studies investigating consciousness through quantum physics. It is successful to some extent but still, science could not find the reason for the survival of consciousness after the brain is shut off.

The real fundamental concept is that we ignore consciousness, and identify ourselves to our body. The body is only a resting place, like an inn. It will perish one day but our pilgrimage is eternal. Being in the body one can become identified, one can start thinking, "I am the body." "I am the mind." This is happening more and more in the modern materialistic world.

According to science, consciousness is an illusion, the body is the only reality. The truth is that the body has its reality, and consciousness has its reality. The miracle is, that these two separate realities are together, and are functioning in deep synchronicity.

As one goes deeper into this philosophy, he will be able to realize that if the hand is cut off, consciousness is not reduced. It remains the same. If the leg is cut off; the body is no longer the same, but his consciousness remains the same. If one's mind changes, his consciousness does not change. It is the only unchanging; everything else is in flux. Only the witness remains permanent and eternal. Mind is time, whereas consciousness is timeless.

Death does not destroy anything. The five elements of the body fall back into their sources and for the consciousness, there are two possibilities: if it has some desires left, it will move into another womb; if it has known its eternity, its immortality, it will move into the cosmos and disappear into this vast existence. He has become one with the source. This is called *Nirvana or Moksha.*

A conscientious person knows there is no death. The Soul is immortal. Death does not happen; it has never happened. It happens only when one is identified with the body and doesn't know himself. Yes, from the body he will be separated, and separation looks like death. But if one is not identified with the body and he knows himself as the witnessing soul, as the pure consciousness, as the pure awareness, then there is no death. It is an interval between the existing life and the next life. In summation, why people do worry about life after death, why don't they enjoy the life they have now and forget the past and the future? On the other hand, if consciousness can survive and act independently of the body during one's lifetime, it can surely survive after death. It is very appropriate to quote here Stanislav Grof, a Czech psychiatrist, "Whether or not we believe in survival of consciousness after death, reincarnation, and karma, it has very serious implications for our behavior."

> "Soul, like the circle, is never ending and
> turn round and round without a stop."
> — *Ravi Puri*

Chapter Nine
Reincarnation and Karma

*"As a man, casting off worn-out garments taketh new ones, so
the dweller in the body, entered into ones that are new."*
— *Bhagavad Gita*

Reincarnation is very concrete proof that consciousness survives death. The human mind is grappled with the notion of reincarnation for millennia. Conviction in reincarnation is as old as humanity's faith in divinity. The overwhelming majority of the earth's inhabitants believe in life after death. The doctrine of reincarnation of the soul is a fundamental dogma of about 5000 years old religion Hinduism. Acceptance of reincarnation is central to Hinduism.

As per Dalai Lama, the spiritual leader of the Tibetan people, "Reincarnation is not an exclusively Hindu and Buddhist concept, but it is part of the history of human origin. It is proof of the mind stream's capacity to retain the knowledge of physical and mental activities. It is related to the theory of independent origination and the law of cause and effect."

The ancient Egyptian and the Greeks also believed in reincarnation. They attributed the concept to an Egyptian mystic known as Thoth Hermes. According to him, "The soul passes from form to form, from level to level, and mansions of its pilgrimage are many." Pythagoras, Plato, Socrates, Aristotle, and Emerson had absolute conviction in this philosophy of reincarnation. Socrates articulated, "I am confident that there truly is such a thing as living again, that the living spring from the dead, and that the souls of the dead are in existence."

Reincarnation was accepted for the first 500 years' history of the church and later was condemned by the Council of Constantinople. Reincarnation is considered by many Christians to be against Christian Doctrine in the United States. About 25 percent of Christians believe in reincarnation. In 1959, Great Britain showed that 12 % of the people believed in reincarnation. The Figures had grown to 28% in 1979. Today, the concept of reincarnation is widely accepted throughout the world.

When we talk about reincarnation, some of the questions perplexed us such as *who are we? Where do we come from? Where do we go from here? Why are we here?* Scientists and philosophers are still struggling to find the answers to these questions. Stuart Hameroff, who proposed the highly controversial Orch-OR (orchestrated objective reduction) theory of consciousness in 1996 along with Roger Penrose, told the *Science* channel, "I think the quantum approach to consciousness can, in principle, explain why we're here and what our purpose is, and also the possibility of life after death, reincarnation and persistence of consciousness after our bodies give up." He has been assiduously working on this subject but nothing conclusive has been revealed so far.

Eben Alexander, a neurosurgeon, wrote the widely circulated and criticized book, *Proof of Heaven.* He described his own experience in this book. He said, "I have a great belief and knowledge that there is a wonderful existence for our souls outside of this earthly realm and that is our true reality, and we all find that out when we leave this earth." Eben Alexander says that he traveled through this heaven, surrounded by "millions of butterflies," with a woman. This woman gave him three messages: "You are loved and cherished, dearly, forever," "You have nothing to fear" and "There is nothing you can do wrong."

Reincarnation studies have been done by Ian Stevenson, Director of the Division of Personality Studies at the University of Virginia. Stevenson has devoted the last forty years to the scientific documentation of past life memories of children from all over the world. He studied over 3,000 cases. Many people, including skeptics and scholars, agree that these cases offer the best evidence for reincarnation.

Near-death experiences (NDE) have been described by patients in hospitals during their surgical operations including the brain, heart attacks, and related critical conditions. Patients have narrated every detail of the actions in the operation theater including the conversations among the nurses and doctors operating upon them. Most of them even saw their body being worked on while standing outside the body.

Birth defects, birthmarks, and fatal wounds like gunshots related to past life have been observed in many people.

Extraordinary qualities or talents in education, music, sports, and acting, such as playing some musical instruments, singing, or knowing some languages, best sportsman at a very young age indicate past life expertise. A Russian lady called Tati Valo claims to have proof of reincarnation. She is said to be able to speak one hundred and twenty languages and believes that many of them are from previous lives. It is not easy to learn so many languages in one life. Suddenly, she remembered all the languages in a mathematics class and completely forgot the Russian language.

Fear of fire, firearm, water, and heights in children and adults relate to the cause of death in their past life. Fear of Fire—if someone died in the fire; firearm— died by gunshot; fear of water—died by drowning; height—died by falling from the cliff or top of a building, etc., etc. Aversion or liking to some foods also refers to past life experiences. Perverted or sexual activities in children at an early age are attributed to their past life habits. Bad habits, stealing, lying, gambling, and strange behavior during early childhood are considered to be the impressions of past life experiences.

Gillian Anderson, an American-British film actress, activist, and writer said, "My whole life belief system is that our paths are drawn for us. I believe in reincarnation. I believe we're here to learn and grow. We choose how we come into this life based on what it is we have to learn. Some people have harder lessons than others."

The word reincarnation means embodiment again, coming again into a physical body. The individual soul takes again a fleshy covering. The word transmigration means passing from one place to another - passing into a new body. It is called *Samsara* in Vedanta.

The Sanskrit term *Samsara* is derived from the Sanskrit root *Sr,* which means - to pass -. The prefix *Sam* means - intensely -. The individual soul passes repeatedly through this world and other subtle higher worlds. This repeated passing of souls - *Samsriti* - is what is really meant by the term *Samsara.* Samsara exists so that the individual soul may learn to realize itself. Paramhansa Yogananda, an Indian yogi, and Guru who introduced millions of westerners to the teachings of meditation and Kriya Yoga through his book, *Autobiography of a Yogi,* said, "Reincarnation is the law of spiritual evolution. It gives everything a chance to work out of its Karma (the law of action). Evolution and reincarnation are methods of propelling all creation towards final freedom in spirit, held no longer under the law of natural law of death."

What is the law that governs transmigration? Is it an automatic system? Who decides that? Some are born into rich families, whereas others are born into poor families. Some are born in rich countries whereas others are born in very poor countries. Some people have a very short life, some have a long life. Some can survive in drastic circumstances whereas others die even in healthy environments. One is born blind. One is born handicapped, the other is born healthy. One is handsome, the other is ugly. One is genius and sharp. One is talented, the other is retarded, and so on. There are lots of disparities. Why? Is there any law that governs life and death? Do human beings come here and pass out without any definite purpose? Is there no role of genetics in these factors?

The cause is the unmanifested condition of the effect whereas the effect is the manifested state of cause. A tree is a cause, and a seed is an effect. The morphological and chemical constituents of a tree: how it looks and what types of phytochemicals are being biosynthesized by it are stored in the tiny seed in potential energy. This tiny seed will give rise to the same physical and chemical properties after it attains the form of a big tree again. The active chemical constituents would almost remain the same. The seed of a mango tree will produce a mango tree only not a banana tree. Similarly, the seeds of the apples will produce an apple tree not a peach tree, and so on. Likewise, the whole human form remains in the drop of semen in an invisible potential form. It produces only a human being nothing else. In the case of a human, its consciousness is in a higher stage. It goes for reincarnation. Within the gross physical human body, there is another subtle body called the astral body. It is invisible and comprises all the impressions and tendencies of the mind.

After the death of the body, the astral body transmigrates to another body with all the impressions of the previous life. This remanifestation of the subtle form into gross physical form is called the law of reincarnation. Every child is born with certain characteristics related to past conscious actions. Goethe, the eminent German poet, was the master of seventeen languages. These cannot be acquired in one life. There must be some effect of previous lives. Similarly, Ludwig Van Beethoven, a German composer, and Pianist was deaf but used to compose extraordinary symphony music.

Likewise, we can make the same statement about eminent scientists, Albert Einstein, Tesla and Edison, and many other born genii. There are many stories such as citing a boy of five who becomes a piano expert. There had been boy-mathematician etc. This is not a miracle of nature but a result of past life and can be explained. If a person gets deep grooves in mind by learning music, musical instruments mathematics, or any medical science in this birth, he or she carries these impressions in the quantum state to the next birth and starts showing extraordinary talents during their childhood.

Heredity and ecological variations can explain certain things but cannot explain all these variations and diversities. Most of the time parents do not possess these qualities. Many intelligent parents have children with dull intellect or vice versa. It is a clear indication of past life experience. If the desires are not fulfilled in this life, the person has to come back again and again to the earth-planet for their fulfillment. If one has an ardent desire to become an actor and could not achieve it and he still cherishes this desire. This desire will bring him back to life and place him in suitable environments and favorable circumstances to become an actor. Now the question arises as to why we do not remember our past. The possible answer is since we pass through many lives, it is not possible to remember any of them. We will go insane if all those memories stay with us in every life. So, Mother Nature concealed the past and kept the mind clean. However, some talents or tendencies from the past lives and will be there to make you an extraordinary scientist, physician, musician, singer or actor or golfer, etc. Most people are born genius.

As per Vedanta, there is a law that governs life and death. This is the law of cause and effect that covers everything, and the entire world runs under this law. The law of Karma is the law of cause and effect. The law of Karma states that your thoughts, words, and actions circle back to determine your future. To every action, there is an equal and opposite reaction. As you sow, so shall you reap. Every effect must have a cause and vice versa. Something cannot come out of anything. Existence cannot come out of nonexistence.

The doctrine of rebirth is a repercussion of the Law of Karma. The differences in personality that are found between one individual, and another must be due to their respective past actions. Past action denotes past birth. Further, all your Karma cannot certainly bear fruit in this life. Therefore, there must be another birth for enjoying the remaining actions. Each soul has a series of births and deaths. Births and deaths will continue until knowledge of the Immortal is attained. Very nicely expressed by Jalaluddin Rumi, a 13th-century Persian Sunni Muslim poet, Islamic scholar, theologian, and Sufi mystic, "I died as a mineral and became a plant, I died as a plant and rose to animal, I died as an animal, and I was Man. Why should I fear? When was I less by dying?"

Good Karma lead to incarnation into higher spheres and bad Karma into lower. If Karma - whether good or bad - are not exhausted, men do not attain the final liberation even in hundreds of births unless knowledge of the eternal is not complete. Both good and bad Karma bind tight the *Atman* in their chains. Some are born with purity and extraordinary talents because they have undergone various disciplines in their past lives. They are born as Avatars such as Jesus Christ, Rama, Krishna, Buddha, and Guru Nanak Dev.

A newborn child manifests marks of joy, fear, and grief. This is inconceivable unless we suppose that the child, perceiving certain things in this life, remembers the corresponding things of the past life. The things which used to excite joy, fear, and grief in the past life, continue to do so in this life. The memory of the past shows the previous birth, as well as the existence of the soul. Michael Ondaatje, a Canadian novelist and poet, voiced on reincarnation, "For the first forty days a child is given dreams of previous lives. Journeys, winding paths, a hundred small lessons and then the past is erased."

Human beings do not come into the world in total forgetfulness and utter darkness. They are born with certain memories and habits acquired in previous births. Desires take their origin from previous experiences. We find that nobody is born without desire. Every being is born with some desires which are associated with the things enjoyed by him in the past life. The desires prove the existence of an individual soul in previous lives. Brian Weiss, an American psychiatrist, hypnotherapist, and celebrated author illustrated the validity of reincarnation in his book, *Many lives, and Many Masters.* His research includes reincarnation, past life regression, future life progression, and survival of the human soul after death. He illustrated, "I think the great lesson for me of all my research and studies is that we do not die when our physical body dies. A part of this goes on as consciousness or soul, or spirit since we are eternal. I believe that a famous mystic summed up a century ago by saying, we are not human beings here having a spiritual experience, but we are spiritual beings having a human experience."

The soul migrates with the astral body. This astral body is made up of nineteen principles, such as five organs of action, five organs of knowledge, five *pranas* (breathing energy) plus mind, intellect, the subconscious mind, and egoism. This subtle body carries with it all sorts of memories, impressions, lust, incomplete desires, or affinities, of the individual soul. The subtle body moves towards heaven. When the fruits of good Karma have been exhausted, it appears in a new physical form and reincarnates on this earth planet.

Those whose actions have been good are born in upright families, and those whose conduct has been evil are thrown into sinful wombs or lower births. This explains the disparities among human beings.

The chains of desires tie us to this wheel of Maya or illusion, a round of births, and deaths. As long as we desire objects of this world, we have to come back to this world in order to possess and enjoy them. But, when all our desires for mundane objects cease, then the chains are broken, and we are free and final liberation is attained.

As lord Krishna said in the Bhagavad Gita, "To the man thinking about the objects (of the senses) arises attachment towards them; from attachment, arises longing; and from longing arises anger. From anger comes delusion; and from delusion loss of memory; from loss of memory, the ruin of discrimination; and on the ruin of discrimination, he perishes."

If we unite ourselves with Him through meditation, and good Karma, and leave our desires, we will obtain immortality and eternal bliss. Bonds of Karma can be cut through knowledge of the Eternal that leads us to absolute bliss and peace. We will be freed from sins, passion, and the cycles of births and deaths.

Zeena Schreck, an American artist, musician, author, and spiritual leader, remarked about the reincarnation of human consciousness, "Consciousness is endless, from one incarnation to the next. It simply will and does manifest in other places and times, regardless of what becomes of the human race." Do animals go through the process of laws of Karma, cause, and effect? There is only one religion, Jainism that believes everything undergoes through the process of reincarnation as animals, plants, insects and even microorganisms' souls can progress from form to form. However, the human race is the one in which the soul can become liberated.

During recent years, there has been a surge of interest in reincarnation especially in Western countries. Celebrities and the younger generation have become captivated by Eastern religious philosophies and practices. Today, there is a plethora of books and Internet sites that discuss the implication of supposed past-life experiences. Past-life regression and treatment are being advertised and people are assiduously following them.

> "Karma is not something complicated, or philosophical.
> Karma means watching your body, watching your mouth,
> and watching your mind. Trying to keep these three
> doors as pure as possible is the practice of karma."
> — *Thubten yeshe*

Chapter Ten
God's Existence: Religion Reflection

*"Atheists who keep asking for evidence of God's existence are
like a fish in the ocean wanting evidence of water."*
—Ray Comfort

Today, the world is passing through a revolution of high
technology. Life is moving very fast. State-of-the-art electronic
devices such as iPods, iPads, kindle, high-speed internet,
artificial intelligence, sophisticated mobile phone, minicomputers,
robots, supersonic jets, and rockets made life very comfortable. Thus,
the distance between the planets has been overcome. Communication
has become easy and rapid through this modern technology.

Despite the dramatic advances in high-technology medicine
such as gene therapy, laser, and plastic surgery, anti-aging devices,
high-resolution body scanning, and scientific miracles like vital
organ transplantation; incredibly, human beings know very little
about their true selves. We have enough knowledge of the various
objects and have made tremendous progress in high tech, artificial
intelligence, and trying hard to explore the universe. We have also
achieved success in these areas to a great extent and even enhanced
life expectancy by prolonging the aging process.

On the other hand, the advancement in technology has resulted
in a rat race of developing superior nuclear weapons throughout the
world. Every country, big or small, rich or poor, wants to be ahead
in this race. This competition, unfortunately, caused a tremendous
amount of physical, emotional, and mental stress. In other words, a
revolution in technology has screwed up humanity.

All over the world, intolerance, crime, corruption, and terrorism
are thriving, and many nations feel insecure among others. Thus, we
are capturing the *outer world* at the cost of the *inner world*. It is very
pertinent to maintain a balance between the *outer* and *inner* worlds
to keep peace in the universe. It is not out of the way to cite Terrence

McKenna, an American ethnobotanist, mystic, and author, "We have been to the moon, we have charted the depth of the ocean and heart of the atom, but we have a fear of looking inward to ourselves because we sense that is where all the contradictions flow together."

Each individual must find the cause of sorrow in his *inner world. Man has become unconsciously cruel, selfish, arrogant, and often behaves sadistically and hysterically.* He is uncouth in his thoughts, low in his morals, and traumatized all around in his capacity to face his personal life and its problems. He lost his self-control. Like an abandoned garden, the inner world has grown into a jungle. Man lives the outer world, from within. If he controls the inner world, the external world cannot influence, how strong it may be. "An individual who has mastered himself is a master of the external world," is an old saying.

The sufferings of the present age are due to one's weaknesses, within. Everyone is a slave to his passion, lust, greed, anger false pride, and intellectual bankruptcy. He is striving hard to gain materialistic comforts at the cost of his inner peace, morals and ethics. Shattered and confused, he cannot face the challenge of the external world. He is like a neglected boat at the mercy of the waves. That is no life.

Among, the world's chaos, intolerance, terrorism, corruption on the rise, and countries at war, if we train ourselves by any technique to live a more definite life of self-mastery that can control our inner world, our external world problems can be mitigated to a great extent. How to control this mental turmoil? The practice of Meditation is the answer. Mediation is one of the techniques that bring a change in the consciousness of the people, which results in the transformation of the entire world. The change in our thinking is very essential if we want to change the modern world. By changing the inner attitude of our minds, we can change the outer aspects of our lives. We need strong motivation and determination. Most people do not want to do meditation because they are not sure about the *Existence of God.* There are several questions on the existence of God even by religious people. Their faith is shaken when they come across mass killings in public places. From time to time, there is always news in the newspaper or on TV of mass killings in schools or shopping centers in the USA. There have been 202 mass shootings based on Gun Violence Archives (GVA) data from January 1 to May 10 (2022). This is on par with data from 2021 during the same period, with 205 mass shootings. Data reviewed by Fox News Digital show mass shootings for the entirety of 2020 increased by more than 40% compared to 2019, according to GVA data, with 417 mass shootings events in 2019 to 611 in 2020. Crime in the USA is increasing day by day. Very recently, on May 24 (2022) an 18-year-old gunman in Uvalde (Texas) killed 19 elementary school children and two teachers.

Texas also had more people killed in mass shootings than any other state, according to data. Innocent people including children are being killed by crazy people. They are killing by the name of religion, race, hate, jealousy, and so on. The phenomenon is spreading like a wildfire throughout the world.

Nevertheless, terrorism is also increasing day by day and these people had even targeted churches, mosques, and temples to create anarchy. The global death toll from terrorism over the past decade ranged from 8000 in 2010 to a high of 44600 in 2014. In 2017 terrorism was responsible for 0.05% of global deaths. Bombs blast events at various shopping centers in different parts of the world are another chaos. Life is not comfortable as it used to be,

In 1990 a big display of terrorism was observed in Kashmir Valley in India which started around 1980. Hindus started plying to other states. They were forced by Muslim terrorists to leave their houses. Scholars and professionals were killed now and then by Muslim terrorists to create fear in the mind of Hindus. Finally, genocide started in 1990 and about 500,000 Hindus were compelled to leave their homes within a few weeks. They were thrown out of their homes in the country where they were living for generations. Those who persisted to stay were killed. Their women and daughters were raped and killed in front of them. It was the biggest massacre after 1947 when the British divided India into Pakistan based on religion.

Kashmir valley was known for literature and art. Most of the holy Hindu scriptures were written over there. Beautiful ancient Hindu temples that were the pride of the Kashmir valley, were destroyed by Muslim terrorists.

The USA did not realize about terrorism until On April 19, 1995, morning, a Ryder truck equipped with a bomb exploded next to the Alfred Murrah Federal Building in Oklahoma City, killing 168 people, many among them innocent children at a daycare center in the building.

September 9, 2011morning shocked the USA, when two planes, hijacked by Islamic jihadists vowing death to all Americans, plowed into both towers at the World Trade Center in New York. Another plane was flown into the Pentagon in Washington, DC. A fourth plane, presumably headed for the White House or the U.S. Capitol, was heroically diverted by passengers and ended up crashing in an empty field in Pennsylvania. After reports of the first plane hitting the North Tower, millions watched the second plane hit the South Tower on live television. About 3000 people were killed in the deadliest terrorist attacks in American history. It was a terrifying, startling, and humbling event for the country.

There are mammoth acts of terrorism that damage economic and intangible assets besides human loss. The year 2014 was marked as the most expensive year for terrorist attacks from all over the world which cost $52.9 billion. Terrorist attacks have been on the rise since the September 11 World Trade Center and Pentagon attacks. (The Price of Terrorism, *Worldatlas.com*).

Countries around the world need to be proactive in their efforts to end terrorism since God is not going to take over. This is man's creation and God has nothing to do with it.

Very recently, the Ukraine war is another example. Russia invaded Ukraine on Feb 24, 2022. It is almost six months have passed. Russia's army has been destroying Ukraine with modern nuclear weapons. They are even killing innocent civilians and raping girls and women irrespective of their ages. Ukraine has turned into ruins. The office of the United Nations High Commissioner for Human Rights verified a total of 5237 civilian deaths as of July 24, 2022. Of them, 348 were children and7035 people were reported to have been injured. Every day, the war takes dozens of civilian lives and the lives of Soldiers. If human life matters, this needs to stop.

When these types of war, crimes, corruption, and holocaust occurred, the *belief in God* is shaken. The idea comes to mind. *Does God Exist?* If there is a God, then why is he not preventing deadly events comprising genocides and atrocities? That means there is no God. Are people worshiping at various religious places Churches, Mosques, and Temples for various reasons wasting their time? If God does not exist then all these religious places should be closed and turned into cinemas, amusing clubs, and sports stadiums. It is not out of the way to quote here Sam Harris, an American non-fiction writer, philosopher, and neuroscientist, "Either God can do nothing to stop catastrophes, or He does not care to or He does not exist. God is either impotent, evil, or imaginary. Take your pick and choose wisely."

There must be something to believe, according to the survey of all recognized religions, it is revealed that God existed but all religions have their definition, explanation, and concept of God. Science is the only one and there is only one truth in science. Whereas religions are many and their myths hardly match each other. It is hard to say how much truth is there in their myths since there is no concrete evidence to prove those. People have debated the existence of God for thousands of years. Most conclusions cannot be proven one way or the other. The majority think the answer lies in abstract philosophy and the metaphysical. Others say, "they do not know" if God exists. Some don't care. Those who do accept His existence often do passively, merely because they were taught it in childhood.

Mostly religion is inherited from family. In other words, it runs in families. Whatever is taught during childhood is exactly engraved in the mind of a child which is very difficult to get rid of it or change to something else. When he grows up his faith gets stronger, and no education or science can change it. A person born in a devoted Christian family or a Hindu or Islamic family will not change his or her religion. The same goes for other religions. If someone changes his religion, it would be circumstantial depending upon his adoption by another religious family or inter-religion marriages. People born in and growing up in a faithless family have no faith in God. The majority stick to religion due to tradition, intimidation, fear, and social pressure.

Another factor that creates doubt about the existence of God is, there is no strong evidence about its existence except it is mentioned in religious sacred scriptures. God exists because the holy scriptures say so. God is an entity whose existence cannot be proven. One must believe in Him. That's all since He is not an object.

Moreover, there is no scientific proof for the existence of things like the soul, the metaphysical, reincarnation, and the presence of hell and heaven. Nevertheless, even God is unpredictable. If something incredible happens, it is a sign of His grace. If something bad happens, then God moves in mysterious ways. Credit or discredit is given to God. The common thinking about God-- God is always looking for every individual in the world and controls everybody's actions. The population of human beings in the world is about 7.80 billion. So, God would be busy all the time taking care of every individual. Believers also claim that God is responsible for everything from birth to death, even choosing, family, place, country, and time of birth and death.

If birth and death are in the hands of God, how come people are killing each other? Some of them are professional killers operating nationally and internationally. Death is in their hands or God's hands. How about assassinations? Abraham Lincoln, John F. Kennedy, Robert Kennedy, Mahatma Gandhi, Martin Luther King Jr., Aldo Moro, Indira Gandhi, Rajiv Gandhi, and many more were assassinated. Is it God's will? How about rapes and murders? How about catastrophes? How about abortions and feticides? Are these occurred by God's will?

Every religion has its concept of God. People perceive it in so many ways. Even in the same religion, they have differences. African American Christians perceive Jesus as black whereas American Christians portray him with blond hair and blue eyes. What was he originally, nobody knew. All his portraits or statues are different. The same types of variations are found in other religions, too. Imaginative statues or paintings of prophets, God, and Goddesses are portrayed and sold at various places of worship. Selling of God is a big market.

Science with advanced technology is improving but religions are almost the same and follow the same old scriptures some are written 5-600 years back. Even the mentality of the followers is not changed rather they are fighting over the interpretation of sacred texts. Recently, killings of Hindus by Muslims have been reported in India based on religion. They were killed in the name of their God, Allah. No religion teaches violence then why killings are being done in the name of God? It reminds the quotes of Karl Marx "Religion is the opium of the people."

So much is going on by the name of God whose existence is questionable since time immemorial. We might live in a modern world, but religion is still pulling plenty of strings out there, and things don't have to be like that. Many people would agree that spiritual matters shouldn't be forced upon the general population and that religious institutions and priests shouldn't be allowed to have any impact on any country's government. Still, these situations are always present around the globe – especially in tempestuous areas where people are very sensitive to religious issues. However, politicians always exploit to gain favors in terms of votes.

Before proving the existence of God, first, we need to understand the true definition of God. There are many Gods and Goddesses in some religions. Those all are His manifestations as explained earlier in chapter three, the Concept of God in various religions. God is one of all religions. Definition of God from most religions. There is only one God. True is His name. He is non-doer, immortal, birthless, formless, and self-illuminated, which means self-created, He is all-knowing, all-knowledgeable, all loving. Omnipresent, omniscient, omnipotent and omniverse. He is true in the prime, true at the beginning of ages, true He is even now, and true He verily, and shall the be in future too. In other words, God is a spirit. He is bodiless, and can't be weighed, can't be measured, can't be touched, or felt. He is beyond time and space and the universe. He is in the present, the past, and the future. He is above all and came from nowhere, Self-created.

He is eternal. Ageless. He knows everything even more than humans. Never learn anything, intellect is infinity. All powerful. He can do whatever he wants, and none can question him. He does everything himself, consults no one, he knows past present, and future. He is holy. glorious, he exists eternity to eternity, He is pure, righteous, in all His ways. God's true characteristics are beyond the imagination of anyone. He cannot be confined to any language, religion, space, and time. He cannot be defined as an individual perception. He is the creator of the universe. He is the past, present, and future. He is eternal and will continue to exist even when there is nothing in the universe. No one who is mortal or undergoing transformation fits into the definition of God. The creator is independent, self-illuminated, and autonomous.

He is immobile and inactive. The true nature of the creator cannot be created by the creation of its creator. The true nature of God and all directly related to Him is pure, complete, without measure and substance. What can we measure, or test is linked to our senses. Sense of creation cannot meet its creator. In the same way, the painting does not know its painter.

Chapter Eleven
Creation of the Universe:
Religion Reflection

"If you want to find the secret of the universe, think in terms of energy, frequency and vibrations."

—*Nikola Tesla*

Creation of the universe is a mystery. How did the universe come into existence? It is a big riddle. Science and religion have been struggling to solve this clandestine since antiquity. Religions from all over the world have tried to explain its mysterious genesis. A Survey of the major religions reveals different interpretations of the creation of the universe. It was, thought, desirable to take a bird's eye view of the origin of the universe through major religions.

Creation of the Universe as per Hinduism:

Hinduism, the oldest and third big religion in the world uniquely describes the creation of the universe. Over 5000 years old Hinduism is the only religion that has the concept of life cycles of the universe. It suggests that the universe undergoes an infinite number of deaths and rebirths. In Hinduism, it is said that the universe is without a beginning (*Anadi*, meaning beginning-less) or an end (*Ananta*, meaning end-less). Also, Hindus believe the universe is projected in cycles. Hindu scriptures refer to time scales that vary from ordinary earth day and night to the day and night of the Brahma which are a few billion earth years old.

According to Hinduism, the universe is the result of the manifestation of God, the supreme consciousness. Before the existence of the universe, there was neither matter nor energy. There was total emptiness alone the one breath, the God. There was neither existence nor nonexistence, neither death nor immortality. There was neither the sign of night nor day, it was total darkness. No sky, no space, no sound, and time. The temperature was zero, with no force or movements, no particles, no liquid, no energy and matter, a state of nothingness meaning the fundamental state of matter known as *Prakriti.*

There was no one to know anything till God created the universe. Then in the beginning God created everything with one word "Om". Word "Om" in Hindu cosmology is considered the first sound of the universe. From the Om, five elements came into existence. The first was space, the shelter of billions of heavenly bodies. From space, it came gas, ranging from light, to heavy. From gas, came fire (plasma). From fire came liquid. And at the end number of heavenly bodies were created. In the tenth book (Mandala) of Rig-Veda, 129th Hymn deals with the origin of the universe and creation which is described below:

"Neither existence nor nonexistence was there. There was neither the realm of space nor the sky beyond.

But for that breathless one breathing on its own. There was nothing else, surely nothing.

Darkness was hidden by darkness in the beginning, with no distinguishing.

In the beginning, all this verily was Atman (Supreme Being) only.

For Om, the five elements came to be; space, air (gas), fire (plasma), water (liquid), and earth (Solid)."

The leading modern theory of the universe "Big Bang Theory" tries to explain the creation of the universe, it also states that there was nothing at the beginning and not a single being existed. All that we now know was compressed into a single dense point known as Singularity.

After the Big Bang, the universe started to expand from that singularity and space came into existence. It is said that during the starting minutes, light elements were born like Deuterium and

Hydrogen. From these light elements, many heavy elements like lithium, potassium and rubidium were formed.

In Hindu cosmology the process of creation and destruction of the universe has no limit, the universe has a specified lifetime and at the end of that time destruction occurs. There is a term "Yuga", in Hindu cosmology, which means the "Ages". Four ages are described in the scriptures, each age possesses a fixed number of years as shown in Figure 2. Golden Age (Satya Yuga); Silver Age (Treta Yuga); Branze Age (Dawaper Yuga), and Iron Age (Kai Yuga). Human consciousness grows and diminishes in cycles. The full yoga cycle is 24,000 divine years, in which period, the Sun makes a full circle around Sirius, 12000 years ascending and 12,000 descending as shown in Figure 2. These four yuga run in the ratio 4,3,2 and 1. Golden is 4,800x360 or 1,728,000 Human years; Silver is, 3600x360 or 1296000 Human years: Bronze is, 2400x360 or 864,000 Human years; and Iron age is 1200x360 or 432,000 Human years. These four Yuga constitute the Mahayuga and are equal to 4.32 million human years. One year of the demigods is equal to 360 years of the human beings. 71Maha Yuga = 1 Manavantara (life span of Manu). There are a total of 14 Manavantara, we are currently in the 7th Manavantara. 14 Manaavanatara are equal to one Kalpa which is a day of Brahma. A Kalpa is equal to 4.32 billion years and measures the duration of the world in its creation and active state. It is believed that the universe is created and destroyed in a cycle every 4.32 billion years. Very interestingly, this period is quite close to the modern scientific age of the earth,

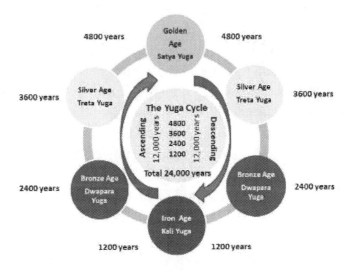

Figure 2: Yuga Cycles

The Veda says that neither non-existence nor existence was there in the beginning. There was no time, no space before the creation. Modern science also agrees with this. There was no sky or atmosphere. What covered this timeless thing? Where, Who, and What was responsible for this?

The Surya Siddhanta (500 BC -800 CE) is the oldest and most incredible Indian text of astronomy with extraordinary knowledge confirming the advanced thinking of the ancient Indians. In this text, one can find the roots of trigonometry, and mathematical inventions, such as standard notation and the decimal system. The text illustrates gravity for a millennium before Sir Isaac Newton developed his theory in 1687. The diameters of the planets are given in this text. The knowledge of modern astronomy was known to sages of ancient India without the powerful Hubble and Web telescopes of today.

The Puranas (Purana means old) were composed by Veda Vyasa around 5000 years ago. Puranas are often dismissed as mere myths. These are a treasure of knowledge. The theory of the creation and expansion of the universe is mentioned in The Puranas. Puranas believed in the one source and the gods in charge of creation, preservation, and dissolution.

The Shrimad Bhagavata Mahapurana even claims that there are multiverses. The timescale description by the ancient Indians is very impressive.

Some western scientists acknowledged the incredible progress of science in recent centuries is greatly inspired by ancient Indian knowledge. Einstein said, "We owe a lot to the Indians." Famous scientists like Heisenberg, Schrödinger, Oppenheimer, and Tesla studied India's ancient wisdom. Robert Oppenheimer, an American physicist, learned the Sanskrit language in 1933 and used to frequently quote the Bhagwat Gita. He used Sanskrit knowledge to decode the Vedas and ancient scripts to form the basis of the Manhattan Project (atomic bomb project). Mark Twain expressed: "Our most valuable and most constructive materials in the history of man are treasured up in India only."

Creation of the Universe: Christianity

According to Christian belief, God created the universe. There are two concepts. Some Christians believe in **Genesis 1.** whereas others in **Genesis 2.**

Genesis 1: *In the beginning, God created the heavens and the earth.* There is no explanation of where God came from. God spoke and the universe came into existence. By faith, we understand that the universe was formed by God's command so that what is seen was not made from what was visible. God created everything by what theologians call *ex nihilo* or "out of nothing". This creative act speaks to attributes of God, such as His eternality, omnipotence, omniscience, and transcendence, just to name a few. God created everything within the span of six literal days.

On the first day light was created, let there be Light.
On the second day - the sky was created.
On the third day - dry land, seas, plants, and trees were created.
On the fourth day - the Sun, Moon, and stars were created.

On the fifth day - creatures that live in the sea and creatures that fly were created.

On the sixth day - animals that live on the land and finally humans, made in the image of God were created.

By day seven, God finished his work of creation and rested, making the seventh day a special holy day.

Genesis 2, some people think the story goes on to give more detail about the creation of humans, seen as two individuals, Adam, and Eve.

Adam was made from 'the dust of the ground when God breathed life into him.' Eve was created out of one of Adam's ribs to provide company and help for Adam. They lived in a special place called the *Garden of Eden*. Both were given the task and responsibility to look after the place that God had created for them.

Most Christens believe that God was responsible for the beginning of the universe – that he set things in motion and oversaw the process. Fundamentalist Christians believe that as the Bible comes directly from God, everything in it must be the exact truth. Anything that contradicts the Bible is wrong.

Creation of the Universe: Islam

The Qur'an does not have a chapter on the genesis of the universe as do the Jewish and Christian scriptures. Many Christians and Jews believe that God created the universe in six days. The Bible and the Qur'an agree that God created the Universe in six days. The six days of creation are not six earthly days, but Eons. Most modern Muslims also believe in the creation of the universe in *six days*. According to Quran, the universe has a beginning and an end. There was nothing before the universe except Allah and He created the complex universe, seen and unseen, the evidence and the speculative, the earth and all that is on it, and everything is in it. He created the heavens that are near and far, the atmosphere and hemisphere, the splatter sphere, and the outer space of stars, planets, and galaxies. He created all of this in detail and diversity in a systematic way that scientific law can be deduced from it, yet so expansive and profound that science is unable to accurately measure or predict. He created the heavens and earth in six periods. He covers the night with the day and then he created the sun, the moon, and the stars. Then He subjected them by his command unquestionably. He is the creator and only the creator. He is the command, and no one shares his command blessed is Allah lord of the worlds. Author of all existence while He is also all compelling.

As per the Quran that the heavens and earth were joined together as one unit following the big explosion. Allah turned to the sky, and it had been a smoke He said to it and the earth, "come together willingly or unwillingly." They said, "we come together and well in obedience." Thus, the elements and what must come from the planets started to cool come together and form into shape following the natural laws that Allah established in the universe. The Quran further states that Allah created the sun, the moon, and the planets each with their courses or orbits. In the Quran, He says, "It is He who created the night and day and the sun and the moon all celestial bodies swim alone each in its rounded course the heaves." The Quran states that Allah created the heavens and the earth and all that is between them in six days while on the surface this might seem similar to the account related in the Bible.

After the creation of the universe, Allah settled himself upon the throne to oversee his work. He says in the Quran He is who created the heavens and the earth in 6 days, He knows what enters within the heart of the earth and what comes forth out of it what comes down from heaven and what mounts up to it and he's with you where you might be and Allah sees well all that you do. The qur'anic account of creation is in line with modern scientific research about the development of the universe and life on earth.

Given the above discussion, God's existence is proven by scripture. Vedas in Hinduism, Bible in Christianity, and Quran in Islam. Authentication of Authors and dates are not mentioned. The existence of scriptures does not automatically prove anything about the accuracy of what the scriptures contain and who has written them. Nevertheless, the scriptures are full of contradictions, and inconsistent myths. These texts are man-made and can be imperfect.

Some miracles prove the existence of God. Such as people surviving accidents and incurable diseases. Where the Sun gets its energy from? Where did the entire universe along a multiverse with all kinds of planets, galaxies, stars, black holes, and nebulae come from? Who does hold the entire universe together? How are the natural laws and forces balanced in space? Where does life come from? Why is only the earth's planet made for human beings? All these queries indicate the presence of God.

Moreover, morality stems from God. Without God, we could not be good people. Religion teaches morals and ethics; Ten Commandments in Christianity, Quran in Islam, and Gita in Hinduism. Belief in God would not be so widespread if God didn't exist. The world population is 7.8 billion. Most of the people are religious. Religion plays a key role in making upright people, their culture, and their nation. After all, there must be some truth in it. If God does not exist, then why so many people have been worshipping Him since time immemorial?

Similarly, consider that many prayers are inherently selfish. While one prays for his or her relative to get a much-needed kidney or liver transplant, someone else is praying for his organ-donor son's life to be spared. Whether one is praying to win a cricket or tennis match, he is also praying for the people on the opposing side to lose. Everybody feels that his problems are more important than others' problems and seeking help from God. This is both selfish and ridiculous considering the unbelievable number of individual complications and concerns of every human being on this planet. What God should do? Whom should he help?

India the sacred and peace-loving land of Rishis and Saints had suffered enormous atrocities, genocides, and rapes of innocent people almost for 800 years during the Mughal period and later under British rule. Invaders robbed India financially, physically, and spiritually. Their original culture was destroyed. Libraries of famous universities like Nalanda were burnt to ashes. Ancient beautiful temples were demolished and replaced by Mosques and churches. Countless Hindus were proselytized to Islam. Most Hindus sacrificed their lives but did not change their religion. No expression can do justice to describe the crimes of these rulers in India.

The sacred land had produced numerous saints among them were a few realized souls like Sant Kabir, Guru Nanak Dev, Sage Valmiki, Goswami Tulsidas, Tuukka Ram, Chaitanya Mahaprabhu, Adi Guru Shankaracharya, Swami Ram Krishan Paramahansa, Maharishi Raman, Swami Vivekananda, Paramahansa Yogananda and many more. These realized souls who were worshiped by the people could not save them from their miseries. Where was God during that time?

Likewise, British rule grew to include large areas of North America, Australia, New Zealand, Asia, and Africa, as well as small parts of Central and South America. People suffered a lot during British rule, too. Similarly, Hitler's holocaust when he decided to exterminate six million Jews for the sake of cleansing the future generations' genetic pools. Where was God during that time?

Also, during Roman Empire, people suffered, and even the noble prophet Jesus Christ was crucified. Where was God at that time? There are numerous examples from history including the First and Second World Wars where innumerable people died and countless suffered financially and physically. No divinity came to their rescue. When these atrocities occur, people lose faith in the Almighty. The majority of religious people worship God for some personal reasons which are plenty and differ from person to person. In short, they think of God as their savior from any kind of trouble. The last resort for their problem is to pray to God for help. If by chance their problems are mitigated or solved to any extent, they would give credit to God. So, their belief is continued and becomes stronger even in despair and disappointment. However, God does not work that way.

God is always there even before the beginning of time and space. He is the creator of the vast universe and multiverse, but he does not interfere with human actions. He has given free will to every human being, and they are responsible for their actions. God is not the cause of atrocities, genocides, and holocausts occurring from time to time in the world. Some are due to man's actions and sometimes owing to natural calamities. God should not be blamed or asked for help. One needs to face his complications by himself.

In summary, no God, or His demigod or prophet can interfere with human affairs or life. The soul, alone, is directly and inevitably responsible for its actions. Each soul has its own journey. God is nonchalant with the creation of the universe or with any pleasant and unpleasant happening in the universe. The universe goes on of its own accord. With present knowledge, God is out of our observative universe. His creative capacity is beyond our imagination. Presently, new images through the James Webb telescope are revealing amazing information that may change the old concept of the universe and the Big Bang theory in the future. The more deeply scientists reveal the secrets of the universe, the more God would disappear from their hearts and minds. However, until now He exists.

> "Peace comes within the souls of men when they realize their oneness with the Universe, when they realize it is everywhere, it is within each one of us."
> — *Black Elk*

Chapter Twelve
Creation of the Universe:
Scientific Reflection

"My experiences with science led me to God. They challenge science to prove the existence of God. But must we really light a candle to see the sun?"

— *Wernher von Braun*

T he origin of the universe is the origin of everything from the tiniest particles to the planets, and stars, to the largest galaxies, and the very existence of space, time, life, and all other forms of matter and energy. The question arose, how did all occur? Multiple scientific theories plus imaginative myths from all over the world have tried to explain its surreptitious genesis. So far, the most widely accepted explanation of the creation of the universe as per science is the Big Bang theory.

Big Bang Theory:

The theory stated that the universe began as infinite hot (around one billion Kelvin degrees) minutes after its birth, as a dense point only a few millimeters wide known as a cosmic egg. 13.7 billion years ago, this tiny cosmic egg violently exploded and from this explosion, all matter, energy, space, and time were created.

The Big Bang resulted in two major stages of the universe's evolution known as the Radiation and Matter eras that shaped the universe. The radiation era is made of smaller stages of epochs that occurred in the universe such as Planck, Grand unified, Inflationary, Quarks, and Hadron.

During **Planck Epoch,** no matter existed at this time. Only energy and the ancestor of the four forces of nature (Gravity, Strong Nuclear, Weak Nuclear, Electromagnetic), the **super-force**, were present. At the end of this stage, a key event occurred. This event split away gravity from the super-force and made way for the next epoch.

The Grand Unification Epoch: It is named after the remaining three unified forces of nature (Strong Nuclear, Weak Nuclear, Electromagnetic). This epoch ended when the **strong** force or strong nuclear, broke away, leading to the next epoch.

The Inflationary Epoch: In this epoch, the Universe rapidly expanded. In an instant, it grew from the size of an atom to that of grapefruit. It was a hot period as the Universe churned with electrons, quarks, and other particles that led to the next epoch.

The Electroweak Epoch: A different event took place in this epoch. Not one, but both remaining forces of nature – electromagnetic and weak nuclear – split off as well.

The Quark Epoch: Around this epoch, all the universe's ingredients were present. Though, it was still a period of high temperatures and density, preventing the formation of subatomic particles.

The Hadron Epoch: During this epoch stage, temperatures started to drop. The universe cooled down enough thus quarks were able to bind together and form protons and neutrons.

The Lepton and Nuclear Epochs: These are the last two stages of the radiation era. During these epochs, the protons and neutrons underwent a significant change – they fused and created nuclei. This led to the creation of the first chemical element in the universe, Helium. The universe's new ability to form elements, the building blocks of matter queued the Matter Era.

Matter Era: as the name suggests, it is defined by the presence of predominance of matter in the universe. It features three epochs that span billions of years.

The first was the *atomic epoch*. In this stage, the temperature cooled down enough for electrons to attach to nuclei for the first time. The process is called *recombination* and resulted in the creation of the second element Hydrogen.

The second is the *Galactic epoch*, hydrogen and helium dotted the universe with atomic clouds. Within the clouds, small pockets of gas may have had enough gravity to cause atoms to collect. These clusters of atoms formed during the galactic epochs became the seedlings of galaxies. Nestled inside those galaxies, stars began to form and in doing so they queued the latest and current stage of the development of the universe.

The third is *Steller Epoch:* At this stage, stars became to form, they caused a tremendous ripple effect and helping shape the universe. Heat within the stars caused the conversion of helium and hydrogen into almost all the remaining elements in the universe as shown in the Periodic Table of Elements.

When a star's core runs out of hydrogen, the star begins to die out. The dying star expands into a red giant, and this now begins to manufacture carbon atoms by fusing helium atoms. There are 116 elements, and out of the 90 are natural.

More massive stars begin a further series of nuclear burning or reaction stages. The elements formed in these stages range from oxygen to iron.

During a supernova, the star releases very large amounts of energy as well as neutrons, which allows elements heavier than iron, such as uranium and gold, to be produced. In the supernova explosion, all these elements are expelled out into space.

Example of Nucleogenesis:

- 3 helium atoms fusing to give a carbon atom: $3 @ {}^4He \rightarrow {}^{12}C$
- carbon atom + helium atom fusing to give an oxygen atom: ${}^{12}C + {}^4He \rightarrow {}^{16}O$
- oxygen atom + helium atom fusing to give a neon atom: ${}^{16}O + {}^4He \rightarrow {}^{20}Ne$
- neon atom + helium atom fusing to give a magnesium atom: ${}^{20}Ne + {}^4He \rightarrow {}^{24}Mg$
- And so on…

In turn, these elements became building blocks for planets, the moon, life, and everything visible today. The sun is the center and around him, the planets revolve in eclipses. The sun itself has a diameter of 866,000 miles. The major planets revolving around the sun are Mercury, Venus, Earth, Mars, Jupiter, Saturn, Uranus, and Neptune. It is interesting to know that earth is suspended in space being held up by the laws of universal gravitation where each planet attracts every other and in return attracted all.

The dominant fundamental force out of the four forces of nature is gravity. Its effects are cumulative. Electromagnetic forces cancel each other with negative and positive charges. The remaining fundamental weak and strong nuclear forces decline with the distance and limit to only the subatomic length scale.

The universe appears to have more matter than antimatter. The imbalance is due to the existence of more matter produced. If the Big Bang produced matter and antimatter equally, photons would prevail as a result of their annihilating interaction. There is no place where the universe began, it happened, everywhere at once.

Size of the Universe: Exact size of the universe is not easy to predict. It does not have a center or an edge. Since we cannot observe the space beyond the edge of the observable universe, it is unknown whether the size of the universe, in its totality, is finite or infinite.

Space, time, and shape: Space and time are an area in which all physical events take place. An event is defined as a unique position at a unique time as such, space-time is the union of all events. No decision on the shape of the universe is made, it can be flat, open, and closed.

Composition of the Universe: 4.9 % ordinary matter, 28.6 dark Matter, 68.3 dark energy. Dark matter and dark energy are invisible. It is hypothetical. The dark energy is spread out throughout space and time uniformly. It has antigravitational properties.

Science cannot explain the complexity and order of life. God must have designed such a complex universe. As per William Paley

(1743-1803) an English Anglican priest, philosopher, and author argued in his book *Natural Theology* that the universe must have been designed by an intelligent creator because it is too complex to have arisen by chance. To illustrate this, he makes an analogy to a watch: if you're walking on the beach and find a watch, you know from its complexity that a watchmaker must have created it. It would be illogical to think that the watch could have dropped spontaneously from the sky. It is a very small example as compared to the creation of the universe. The visible universe is a very complex creation comprising stars, planets, galaxies, and many unknown objects yet to identify. Above all, they are in equilibrium and obey the law of nature. There is some supernatural force that is keeping them in balance.

What is the ultimate end of the universe?

Some say the world will end in fire, others say in Ice. Scientists think that the expansion of the universe ultimately makes it cool as it expands, and the universe may die. The entropy in an isolated system will continuously increase until it reaches a maximum value. At that point, heat in the system will be evenly distributed no room for usable energy (heat) to exist. Mechanical motion in the system will no longer be possible. This theory is named as Big Freeze Theory which is also known as the Heat Death.

There is another version of the ultimate ecological catastrophe of the universe is Vacuum Decay Theory. A change in the energy level of Higg's field would cause a bubble to expand throughout the universe at the speed of light rewriting the nature of the quantum field as it passes and destroying the universe in no time.

Another popular theory is an expansion of the universe will ultimately be reversed at some point and begin to contract. This contraction will cause everything to collapse into a single point which may explode again and result in another Big Bang. This is known as Big Crunch Theory. This also holds that the universe has experienced this transformation an infinite number of times already and it will continue to do so forever. In other words, the universe exists for eternity, but it expands and collapses at different intervals with a huge explosion punctuating each cycle.

This analogy resembles the concept of the creation of the universe in Hinduism. Rig Veda mentioned the universe is a continuous cycle of creation, preservation, and destruction. There is no beginning and there is no end.

So, the universe is not quite as you thought it was.
You would better arrange your belief, then. Because
you certainly can't rearrange the universe.
—*Isaac Asimov*

Chapter Thirteen
The Creator and The Universe

"The Universe is full of magical things patiently waiting for our wits to grow sharper."

—*Eden Phillpotts*

Who has created the Universe? It has been a matter of great controversy since its conception. People have debated the existence of the universe for thousands of years. Religions have their myths (Chapter Ten) and science has its explanations (Chapter twelve). The controversy is going on since antiquity. Religion could not prove the existence of God and science could not disprove it. Let us discuss the creation of the universe from the perspectives of science and religion taking into consideration certain facts.

The previous chapter describes the creation of the universe through scientific reflection. After the occurrence of the Big Bang, the matter was formed following the Radiation Era. The matter and energy were scattered in an orderly manner. So, the universe has a beginning. Now the question arises: *What force could have caused the great explosion leading to the Big Bang and resulted in a universe that did not exist before? What was there before the Big Bang? There should be something. Where did the cosmic egg come from?* Something cannot come from anything; nothing comes from nothing. Ex nihilo nihil (nothing comes from nothing). The universe is the sum of all-natural and physical things. If anything existed before the appearance of the universe, it cannot be part of the universe. It must come from a supernatural trans-physical being. Many scientists supported the existence of a creator having supernatural power one of them was Hugh Ross, an American astrophysicist. He articulated, "By definition, time is that dimension in which cause-and-effect phenomenon takes place. No time, no cause and effect. If time's beginning is concurrent with the beginning of the universe, as the space-time theorem says, then the cause of the universe must be some entity operating in a time dimension completely independent of and pre-existent to the time dimension of the cosmos. It tells us that the Creator is transcendent, operating beyond the dimensional limits of the universe. It tells us that God is not the universe itself, nor is God contained within the universe."

That cosmic egg or small singularity is supernatural which created the world. It is strong evidence of supernatural power or God. If there is a beginning, there must be a beginner. Before the Big Bang, there was nothing except darkness. No sound, no light, no wind, no matter, no energy and Zero Volume. Matter and energy cannot come into existence just like that. It is scientifically impossible. How did this cosmic egg appear? There can be three suppositions.

Let us suppose, everything came into existence by itself, without the help of any power. This is not possible.

Secondly, everything in the universe has *always* existed for all of eternity. According to the *Law of Conservation of Energy, Energy can neither be created nor be destroyed.* Although it may be transformed from one form to another. The Sum of the total remains the same. This can be possible. The universe has been eternal and there is no Big Bang. According to the Big Bang theory, the universe is finite, not eternal. As per the new and recent observations of the James Web Telescope, the Big Bang theory is in Jeopardy. Information collected by JWT challenges the occurrence of the Big Bang.

Thirdly, there must be a supernatural power, that created the Laws of Nature. The most widely accepted supposition is the last one. There is an intelligent creator who created the universe. The universe is huge and comprises trillions of stars, galaxies, black holes, nebulae, planets, multiverse parallel universes, and many more unknown objects beyond our imagination even. What is being perceived by the observers with the latest technology is 5 % of it. Ninety-five percent comprises dark energy (67%) and dark matter (28%). The Composition of Dark energy and dark matter is unknown.

Nevertheless, all these planets, stars, and galaxies are in equilibrium along with the forces acting upon them such as electromagnetic, nuclear, gravitational, and expansion forces. If any of these forces is less or more, it would be chaos. If gravity is more, the expansion would be less and vice versa. The sun generates the right amount of heat and light for the earth's planet. Had the earth bit closer to the sun, lives on earth would have been burnt. Had the earth been too far away from the sun, lives would have frozen. Earth will become a cold desert too. Various gases present on the earth may also lead to an explosion due to rapid contraction and pressure differences caused by the cold temperature.

Sun and moon of different sizes are the perfect distance from the earth, so they appear identical in size from our perspective. Therefore, the moon covers the sun exactly during the solar eclipse. It is amazing and reveals another clue for intelligent design.

When the objects are so fine-tuned and complex in design, it points out the origin of an intelligent designer. Focuses on the evidence of harmony, order, and design in the universe, and argues that its design gives evidence of an intelligent purpose and creator.

If the universe was created by some cataclysmic explosion (Big Bang) then it is reasonable to expect that matter should have been scattered everywhere at random. There would have been chaos. But it is not. Instead, it is organized into planets, stars, galaxies, clusters of galaxies and superclusters of galaxies. Fred Hoyer, a staunch opponent of the Big Bang theory articulated, "The Big Bang theory holds that the universe began with a single explosion. Yet as can be seen below, an explosion merely throws matter apart, while the Big Bang has mysteriously produced the opposite effect -- with matter clumping together in the form of galaxies." On the contrary, the universe operates ordinarily and adheres to multiple laws. It is indeed an extraordinary event and indicates the presence of transcendental power."

The reason why the universe obeys the law of gravity, energy, and fundamental forces- electromagnetic Forces (EMF) weak and strong nuclear forces is because it was designed by a logical and orderly, supernatural power. Four fundamental forces are constant throughout the universe and affect all physical objects everywhere.

Four Fundamental Forces:

Strong nuclear force
Weak nuclear force
Electromagnetic force
Gravitational force

The difference between the strongest and the weakest force is very significant. The molecular biologist Michael Denton has explained very clearly in his book *Nature's Destiny*, the significance of these forces. According to Denton, the Universe was created and specially designed to make human life possible. If these various forces and constants did not precisely have the values they do, there would be no stars, no supernovae, no planets, no atoms, and no life.

The strong nuclear force binds subatomic particles, neutrons, and protons together with the nuclei of atoms. If this force was stronger or weaker by more than one percent, the universe would be either all hydrogen or have no hydrogen at all. It will make the universe a very dull place.

The weaker nucleus force makes radioactive decay, fission, and fusion possible. If this force is a bit stronger or weaker, the universe would have produced far too little or far too much helium in its early history either way. There would be not any planet.

Electromagnetic force binds electrons to the nuclei of atoms. If this force is slightly weaker, the electrons would fly away. If the EMF is slightly stronger, atoms could not share electrons and again and no molecule, not an attractive option for life. First, for life on earth to exist, molecules must exist, and for molecules to exist, atoms must be able to bond to become molecules. This molecular bonding requires just the right amount of electromagnetic force. If this force were only slightly stronger or weaker than molecules could not be formed, and life would have not existed on earth.

If the gravitational force was stronger, stars be so hot, they would burn too quickly. If the earth's gravity is 5% stronger, this will wrap up the earth's planet near-perfect circular orbit into a tighter elliptical path. The earth's core would collapse and destroy everything. It would be a disaster resulting in the end of the planet earth.

If gravity is weaker, stars would not become hot enough to ignite nuclear fusion. Such stars would burn quietly for a long time but make no heavy elements needed for planets. All these forces are interrelated and make our universe the most interesting place to live in as it is. There is some supernatural power that runs the entire balance.

The existence of the universe itself depends on its expansion rate. If the expansion rate of the universe were 1 in 10^55 faster or slower, the universe either would have immediately collapsed in on itself or it would have spun off so fast that there would have been no gigantic formation at all. Another option is, the universe remains the same with too little expansion. Recently, James Webb Telescopes observes so.

World-famous physicist Michio Kaku claims the existence of God. He says, "I have concluded that we are in a world made by rules created by an intelligence ... Believe me, everything that we call chance today won't make sense anymore. To me, it is clear that we exist in a plan which is governed by rules that were created, shaped by a universal intelligence and not by chance." Albert Einstein held some of the same beliefs as Michio Kaku – that the universe is a sign of an intelligent creator.

The next proof of the existence of God is the Law of Biogenesis. Life only comes from life, not from nonliving. Apple produces apple. Chicken produces chicken. Dog produces dog. From where does life originate? How life came into existence from non-life abiogenesis is still a great dilemma. Even the formation of a single cell is a miracle of nature. Even on a planet with the perfect external conditions for life, naturalistic science cannot explain how life began. Before publicizing any theory of natural selection or evolution, one must deal with the *origin* of life. Yet even a single cell is so complex that it defies the possibility that such a thing could simply emerge from primordial slime. There are 2000 types of proteins in a simple bacterium. The probability of their all coming into existence by accident is very rare. In a human being, there are 200,000 types of proteins. So, the question does not arise such an event occurring by chance.

Even if one could synthesize both proteins and DNA, one is still not anywhere close to having a cell. The minimum genome size requires the simultaneous occurrence of all the essential gene products. RNA, DNA, and complex carbohydrates must all be present to form the cell wall, and lipids must be present to form the membrane. There can be no proteins without DNA and RNA, but there can be no DNA and RNA without proteins—and so it goes, on and on and on.

Finally, cells contain *information*. DNA most closely resembles a language because it encodes all the information necessary for life. The information in any human's 70-plus trillion cells is huge. Where does all this information come from? What makes a message? If it represents something other than itself, it requires a speaker—which is a transmitter—and a listener—which is a receiver—and it contains the elements of language.

The presence of all this *information* implies a source of *intelligence*. Information requires intentionality. It does not come about by a random process. Information transcends matter and energy. The pure naturalist will try to imagine a message that does not have a mind behind it, or information that does not have intelligence behind it, but this fact remains: There is only one principle that we know can come up with complex interactive systems, and that is intelligence. This is the explanation most compatible with observable facts.

Another proof of God's Existence is the Law of Cause and Effect. Every known thing in the universe has a cause. Therefore, it reasons, the universe itself must also have a cause, and the cause of such a great universe can only be Good Moral Laws demand which is also the proof of His existence. Moral laws come through consciousness which is also the gift of God.

Free will exists and is also a gift from God. There must be God if there is free will. What human beings do with their free will depends upon their choice of good or bad actions. Good actions lead to rewards whereas bad actions result in punishment. What goes around, comes around.

Above all, the great proof of His existence is the Consciousness that prevails in all living organisms. Human consciousness gives rise to reasoning. The intelligence, and ability to correlate and take decisions and modify behavior according to circumstances. All these come from God. Consciousness intervention can change the shape of the universe. Consciousness is the ultimate reality. The universe is the ocean of absolute consciousness. Each drop of it prevails in living and nonliving matter of the universe and finally comes back to the ocean of consciousness. We are all connected through that absolute consciousness. Consciousness is the only supreme energy that exists, the rest is all illusion.

Many people believe that science can eradicate the need for God. It is not possible. The truth is that all the scientific studies carried out so far have not proven or disproven the existence of God. God is not a matter which can be identified. God is metaphysical, beyond time and space. God is a spiritual being and is outside the reach of empirical scientific research. Religion cannot prove the existence of God with absolute certainty, nor can science disprove his existence with any certainty.

The great ancestors of modern science—Cark Sagan. Max Planck, Nikola Tesla, Albert Einstein, Copernicus, Erwin Schrodinger, Galileo, Blaise Pascal, and Isaac Newton—all professed and believed in God and viewed their scientific studies as a mode of worship.

As per the fundamental definition of God, He is invisible. How can one see or observe an invisible metaphor? One can feel his presence observing the entire universe. Holy scriptures described by the prophets without the help of Hubble or James telescopes are amazing. The creation of the universe described in Rig Veda is astonishing. As per Rig Veda, the creation, preservation, and destruction of the universe is a continuous process. There is no beginning and there is no end. The universe runs in cycles. It is difficult to deny the existence of Almighty God under any circumstances which is the ultimate truth. There is no discordancy between science and religion either. Both are seeking the same truth. It reminds the expression of the great scientist Louis Pasteur, "A little science estranges man from God, but much science leads them back to Him."

> "Everything in this universe is Energy. Trust the Energy you feel around a person. This energy lets you know a lot of information. Listen up!"
> — *Karen Salmansohn*

Chapter Fourteen
God's Existence & the
Kardashev Scale

"Two possibilities are there: either we are alone in the Universe,
or we are not. Both are equally terrifying."

—*Arthur C. Clarke*

T he definition of God fits into that of Energy. Energy can neither be created nor destroyed. It is invisible and formless. It is omnipresent, and omnipotent. It is beginningless and endless. The Kardashev scale at the Type 7 level of energy consists of all the characteristics of the unknown creator. Let us analyze the Kardashev scale from that perspective.

There may be about 40 billion planets that could sustain life in the milky way of our home galaxy. There are countless galaxies like the milky way within the universe. So, there may be countless planets that sustain life. Incredibly, there would not be other intelligent life in the universe. Our civilization may not have been the first intelligent civilization in the universe. The question arises. How to find them? It would be hard to envisage their level of science and technology. Some could have existed for hundreds of millions or billions of years.

Kardashev C. Nikolai, a Russian astronomer who was looking for extraterrestrial life within cosmic signals quantified the amount of energy consumed by civilization in the year 1964. He used this as an indicator in classifying possible alien civilizations. This method of classification is today called the Kardashev scale. He illustrated three Types of civilizations, Type 1, 10^{16} W; Type 2, 10^{26} W; and Type 3, 10^{36} W. W stands for watts. Kardashev originally envisioned only three types of civilizations, but more were later added on. Figure 3 illustrates Type 1 to 7 civilizations.

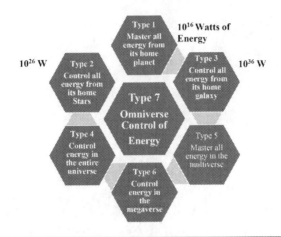

Figure 3: The Kardashev Scale of Advanced Civilizations

Kardashev postulated that there could be an alien civilization that was billions or even trillions of years old. He classified civilizations by level of technological advancement. According to him, a civilization would require energy above all else to develop. Energy is of course required to maintain life but development in science and technology also requires enormous amounts of energy. A civilization that produces more energy could be classified as a more advanced type of civilization.

Type 0 Civilization uses natural resources found on their local planets to obtain energy. It uses resources other than trees such as soot, oil, or natural gases. One characteristic of Type 0 civilization is that it either has not developed propulsor technology, or generators power for all its propulsors by burning chemical fuel. It can also be described as a baby civilization of alien civilization. In the Kardashev scale, the type of civilization is determined based on the amount of energy produced per second. According to the calculation of astronomers, our global civilization would be at Type 0.72 on the Kar scale based on the total energy we consumed. It will take 100 to 200 years for our civilization to increase from a Type of 0.72 to 1.0. The way the progress is being made; it will not take that much time.

A Type 1 Civilization produces at least ten to 16 power watts of energy per second. It is also called a *Planetary Civilization.* It does not depend upon natural resources instead the main source would be nuclear energy. A Type 1 civilization would instead use nuclear fusion. If we could develop the ability to make use of nuclear fusion, we could obtain clean safe and nearly unlimited nuclear energy. Propulsors used within Type1 civilization would be powered by nuclear energy. Once we become a Type 1 civilization, we could be able to send manned spacecraft to near planets in the solar system. Our advanced science and tech would eliminate cancer and other incurable diseases caused by viruses and infections, and developments in regenerative medicine would allow us to regenerate any organ. This would increase our lifespan. We would be capable of living in the sea and the clouds, in addition to on land.

It would take 3000 years to go from an early Type 1 civilization to an advanced Type 1 civilization. Type 1 civilization can harness all kinds of energy on a planet with 100% efficiency. They can harness all forms of energy like hydro, wind, solar, geothermal, coal, oil, nuclear, etc. energies. Human civilization hasn't reached this level yet. Even after achieving these many advances, only 22 % of solar energy could be harnessed.

Our civilization would have access to energy between $10^{16} - 10^{17}$ watts. To have such an energy level, fusion energy, and access to energy from antimatter are required. Type 1 civilization would do this on their planet itself. We would need to boost our current energy production over 100,000 times to reach this status. However, being able to harness all of Earth's energy would also mean that we could have control over all natural forces. Human beings could control volcanoes, the weather, and even earthquakes. We are progressing to get to that level. Internet connection to the world, digital currency, space tourism, exploring life on other planets, and sending satellites to the moon and Mars are the burning examples of our growth. One day, we will reach Type 1 civilization. The Kardashev number for type 1 civilization must be at least 1.16.

Type 2 Civilization is to harness energy from its home star system. This civilization would have access to the energy of the order of 10^{26} **watts** at any point in time. They would be able to construct hypothetical structures like Dyson Sphere, Dyson swarm, and Matrioshka brain. Type 2 civilization would need to have a Kardashev number of at least 1.86.

Dyson Sphere: It is a hypothetical superstructure built around the sun to harness a large part of the sun's energy and divert it back to the earth. This would harvest so much energy that human beings could manipulate and control all natural forces required for Type 1 civilization. Human civilization is just able to launch small satellites into the Sun till now. They need to work on the Dyson Sphere.

Dyson Swarm: Many small energy harvesting units densely clustered around the sun constitute a Dyson Swarm. Dyson Swarm seems to be a little realistic and possible thing when compared to the Dyson Sphere. There are many variants of this Dyson concept.

Matrioshka brain: This is precisely a computer that would harness power from something like a Dyson Sphere and would give enormous computational power to the civilization. They would probably be able to harness energy from Black holes by collecting photons emitted by them. It is possible to harness energy from black holes also.

Type 3 Civilization: Type 3 civilization would use various techniques used by Type 2 at the level of their galaxy which means that they would be able to harness almost all the energy of their home galaxy. They would be able to collect energy from supermassive black holes, gamma bursts, and quasars. This civilization would have access to the energy of the order of 10^{37} watts at any point in time. About 10 billion times the energy output of a Type 2 civilization. Type 3 should have a Kardashev number of at least 2.9

They would be able to extract energy from almost all the galaxy by building something like a Dyson Sphere around them. But stretching over the galaxy in such a manner would face several problems such as the species would be controlled by the laws of physics. Particularly, light-speed travel.

Kardashev thought a Type 4 Civilization was 'too' advanced and didn't go beyond Type 3 on his scale. He assumed that Type 3 would be the extent of progress. But a few believe there can be additional Types of civilization that could be achieved. So, his scale was further extended to seven.

Now for Type 4 civilization energy will be accumulated from each galactic supercluster. Each galaxy will be in a Dyson sphere. This civilization would be supergalactic, able to travel throughout the entire universe and consume the energy output of several galaxies. In other words, control all the energy of the universe. Type 4 civilizations would almost be able to harness the energy content of the entire universe and with that, they could traverse the accelerating expansion of space. Furthermore, advanced races of these species may live inside supermassive black holes. To previous methods of generating energy, these kinds of accomplishments are considered implausible. This civilization would need to tap into energy sources unknown to us using strange, or currently unknown, laws of physics. This means that a Type 4 civilization would have a Kardashev number of at least 4.4.

Type 5 Civilization can harness the energy of the multiverse universe. Each micron will be harnessed to get energy. This infinite amount of energy will not only be cultivated but will be used to change the laws of physics. Type 5 might just be the next possible advancement to such a civilization which can travel to parallel universes, simulate universes, and manipulate reality. Here beings would be like gods, have knowledge, and manipulate the universe as they please. Humans are a very long way from ever reaching anything like this. But it's not impossible. It can be achieved with continued efforts and supports for scientific advances and discoveries.

Type 6 Civilization seems even more unrealistic and bigger than any science fiction movie. The incredibility can be understood by the fact that humans will be able to light the stars. Type 6 will exist outside of time and space, and humans will be capable of creating universes and multiverses and destroying them easily. Humanity will be able to control anything and everything. At this stage, we will practically be Gods, all-seeing knowing. Type 5 civilization will be beneath it and fully at its mercy. This is the topmost level of life, the final boss of existence, the ultimate enforcement of all things. So, what if humanity reached this point? Humanity would not be the same anymore. To reach the present scale of 0.72 to Type 6 civilization would be a great achievement. Right now, we are struggling to make the best use of just one planet, one star, one galaxy, and one universe. To achieve Type 6 civilization we must iron out every single inefficiency from Type1-5 civilization. Take language as a specific example, a Type 6 civilization socially merges not even have one, or at least they would not be communicating in a way that's at all recognizable to us.

At one time in the past, at a lower level of the Kardashev Scale, such a civilization might have amalgamated all previous languages into a universal language. It might then have converted that spoken language into a digital one, negating the need for anything like conversation and avoiding the possibility of miscommunication and confusion. This digital language might then have optimized to something like thought transfer so that not even body language was needed anymore. Thought transfer could lead to the creation of a shared mind. Finally, Type 6 civilization breaks the bondage of even time, space, and reality. The mind becomes more like a chip, ready to assess when needed. Almost all questions will be answered. Can we reach this stage? Appears to be impossible. We can't even imagine this kind of amazing power since we are struggling to ensure our longtime survival on this planet for the time being. If Type 6 civilization is achieved, it will be a heaven on earth.

Type 7 Civilization. Omniverse- since there can be nothing beyond Him. There is only one omniverse (all multiverse). It is a single identity that controls everything there is or can be. Thus omnipotent, omnipresent, and omniscient. To many, this would be God, the creator of all things. It would be responsible for all existence including every timeline of the past, present, and future. Like Type 6 civilization, this being has absolute knowledge of everything. However, unlike Type 6 civilization, it would not need to formulate any further questions since everything for this just be any questions, answers knowns, and unknowns would all just be here in the omniverse as a part of being. It knows everything always. Nothing can be hidden from Type 7 civilization, and nothing can be beyond it. It is the absolute level that anyone could ever hope to achieve. Can humanity reach this level? At this point, no one can answer. Is any of these levels even real? The probability of reaching humanity even at the second level is very small. Will this theory only remain a theory? Physicist and futurist Michio Kaku suggested that, if humans increase their energy consumption at an average rate of 3 percent each year, we may attain Type1 status in 100–200 years, Type 2 status in a few thousand years, and Type 3 status in 100,000 to a million years.

Holy scriptures of the oldest religion in the world Hinduism, indicate the possibility of knowing all these Levels of civilization before the discovery of the Kardashev scale. Airplanes and flying chariots are mentioned in their scriptures. Visits of Sage Narada Muni to different planets are also cited. He could travel to Moon, Mars, and Heaven. How people used to travel to Moon and Mars at that time is not indicated. If we travel thousands of years back, the trail gets difficult to follow but there are still stories, superstitions and legends passed down that show past groups intending concepts like or very close to Kardashev's imagination.

According to some interpretations of ancient Hindu scripture, there is mention of flying machines the importance of stars, the potential for immortality, and even of time travel. The *Vimana* frequently appear in epic Sanskrit poems, as flying chariots, or sometimes as flying temples, they have before been described as early as predictions of today's Jumbo Jets. But, while some of our planes can rival a temple in terms of size, the *Vimana* appears something more advanced like a spaceship, Anyway, these machines link earth to heaven.

Ribhus are depicted as stars. There are three of them altogether, and they are often described as artisans. They were gifted creators, impressing the Gods with their miraculous inventions and abilities including the creation of flying machines. But the Ribhus were also framed for restoring youth to their parents. The idea of immortality is being handled by star-fueled master creators in ancient legend, too. In Soma, the myths of the past include a substance of the future as well. Soma appears in some of the earliest Hindu texts available, as a mystical potion made of unknown ingredients gifted with divine power and knowledge. The exact effect of Soma is known as the elixir of life. Soma grants the drinker with immortality, increased strength, and pure thoughts. Soma was used in magico-religious ceremonies of the Aryans who came to the Indus Valley 6000 years ago. These early invaders of India worshiped the holy inebriant and drank the extract of it in their most sacred rites. An ancient Indian tradition recorded in the Rig Veda asserts that *Parjanya, the God of thunder, was the father of Soma.* Soma is personified by the god Soma who is the God of sacrifices and who may be associated with the Moon. The drink is described and praised in the sacred Rig Veda. Out of the 1000 hymns in Rig-Veda, 120 are devoted exclusively to Soma. In mythology, the god Soma gained immortality by drinking Soma and it was the favorite tipple of God, Indra.

No information about Soma was found in the literature except it is a plant product. The cult died out, and the original holy plant was forgotten. The identity of Soma remained one of the enigmas of ethnobotany for 2000 years. In 1968, some studies carried out and found the major ingredient of Soma could be *Amanita muscaria,* a well-known hallucinogenic. Some mentioned it is a cocktail of hallucinogenic mushrooms, honey, cannabis, blue lotus milk, and pomegranate. Truly speaking, the identity and composition of the Soma drink are still unknown.

In addition to flying machines, star power, and immortality, the ancient texts cover time travel, too. Time moves differently for the Gods than it does for mere mortals on Earth, too, with the highest powers experiencing whole cycles of hundreds of thousands of years, The best example of time travel in Hindu Scripture, is of King

Kakudmi and his daughter Revati. The king sought help from the creator God Brahma, in finding a husband for her daughter, Revati. They could not find a suitable match on earth. They both went to Brahma on a higher level of existence and spent some time there. On their return, they found their kingdom changed beyond their recognition though they spent a few moments with Brahma. Earth was thousands of years older than when they left.

Bhagavata Purana refers to the world of micro and multiverse, too on concepts that have been spoken about at length by modern scientists in the last few years. The text says there are innumerable universes besides this one that moves about the atoms in you. It also refers to countless universes each covered in its own shell and compelled by the wheel of time. The many worlds interpretation argues that some worlds and universes exist parallel in space and time to us. Thinkers now describe the universe as inevitable. The Yuga cycle is equal to 4.5 billion. Earth is also 4.5 billion old. As per Carl Sagan, the Hindu religion is the only religion in which time scales correspond to modern cosmology. Erwin Schrodinger, a Noble Laureate, deeply studied the Hindu holy scriptures and strongly believed in them.

Likewise, Max Muller's, the German philologist and Orientalist spent most of his life in England. He compiled a Sanskrit edition of the Rig Veda between 1849 and 1874. He also published an English version of Rig Veda in 1859. He translated the creation of the universe from Rig-Veda (Mandala 10, hymn129). It is a beautiful description of the Creation of the Universe and explained the preexisting conditions before the formation of the universe.

The speed of Technology Evolution and Development has only gone higher and is progressively increasing at a fast pace besides many problems of wars, floods, earthquakes, diseases, poverty, and environmental destruction. During recent years technology has made tremendous progress starting from organ transplantation, cosmetic surgery, nanomedicine, artificial intelligence, smart toilets, smart mirrors, automatic cars without drivers, deep fake technology, sonic fire extinguisher, quantum computers, GPS- 3 navigation systems, robot soldiers, and space travels and trying for space colonization. Nobody can predict the future. Humanity can achieve marvelous things and it is hoped that the journey continues to reach Type 1 of the Kardashev scale soon.

"A person becomes 10 times more attractive not by his look but by his act of kindness, love, respect, honesty, and loyalty he shows to others."
—*Anonymous*

Chapter Fifteen
The Quest for the Unknown

"The Quest of the Absolute leads into the four-dimensional world."

— *Arthur Eddington*

People are very inquisitive to know the answers to certain questions pertaining to the subject of the text. Efforts have been made to satisfy them.

Q; What is God?
A: God is a concept of some superhuman being who created the Universe and is more powerful. We have essentially created God in our image.

Q: What are the characteristics of God?
A: He is omnipresent, omniscient, and omnipotent. He is Self-created, formless, birthless, and deathless.

Q: Out of what does God create the universe?
A: God is not only intelligent that shapes the universe, but also the material out of which it is made. In this way, God does not stand apart from the creation. God is the very creation itself: the sum of all things seen and unseen.

Q: How God can be the material and creator?
A: Think of the spider. A sider not only makes his web but also provides the material to create such a beautiful design of the web. Similarly, God is the creative principle that shapes and governs the laws of the universe and also the very material out of which it forms,

Q: If God exists, then why does not He protect us from war, genocides, violence, atrocities, and ecological destruction?
A: Human species has been gifted with free will. If we violate the moral law for the sake of satisfying one's desires and aversions, it will

result in suffering. The root of our suffering on a personal and global scale, and the true cause of man's inhumanity to man, is ignorance of our true nature and the nature of reality. So, all these wars, genocides, and atrocities are not caused by God, but by human action, and God is not responsible. Evil is born from the ignorance of mankind.

Q: What is the ultimate Reality?
A: Only the formless *Self* is the ultimate reality

Q: If God Created the universe who created God?
A: God is self-created and self-illuminated. Nobody created Him.

Q: Where did God come from?
A: He is eternal and infinite. He has been there before the beginning of the universe and would be there after the end of the universe. He is beyond time and space.

Q: Does God Exist?
A: It depends upon your belief. His existence is in your thoughts. if you believe He exists, then He does. If not, He does not exist.

Q: What is Space?
A: Where there is an extension, there is space.

Q: What is Time?
A: Time is the perception of the duration of change. Where there is a sequence of events there is time. Time is that dimension in which cause and effect phenomena take place. No time, no cause and effect.

Q: Why don't scientists believe in God?
A: A Pew survey taken in 2009 records that 33 percent of scientists believe in God and another 18 percent in a higher power, compared to 94 percent of the public. So, 51 percent of scientists believe in God. Others deny His existence because of a commitment to materialism.

Q: Can the existence of God be proven?
A: There are only two choices, the eternal universe, or the eternal Creator. The universe is not eternal has been proven by science through the Big Bang and the expansion of the universe. Therefore, an eternal creator exists.

Q: What is the proof of the Big Bang?
A: The radiation echo of the Big Bang.

Q: What is the Big Bang?
A: Around 13.82 billion years ago, everything in the entire universe was condensed in an infinitesimally small singularity, a point of denseness and heat. Suddenly, an explosive expansion began, ballooning the universe outwards faster than the speed of light. This explosion is called the Big Bang, which ultimately resulted in the formation of our universe comprising stars, galaxies, and planets.

Q: What happened before the Big Bang?
A: All the matter and energy were concentrated to a singularity.

Q: When will the time end?
A: Time requires consciousness. If there is an observer, time exists. If there is no observer, there is no time. Also, time is the perception of change. If there is no change, there is no time. Time started with the beginning of the universe, 13.8 billion ago, and will end with the universe.

Q: What is the expanding universe expanding into?
A: We are part of the universe and do not know. Also, according to James Webb space telescope expansion is questionable.

Q: What is Cataclysmic explosion?
A: A sudden and violent explosion. A cataclysmic event changes a situation critically in an unpleasant way.

Q: What is Cosmic Background Radiation?
A: The fossil Electromagnetic Radiation or leftover radiation from the Big Bang or the time when the universe began. It is considered an echo or shockwave of the Big Bang and can be detected by Hubble or James Webb Space Telescopes.

Q: What is Anthropic Principle?
A: It comprises every detail in the universe that has been carefully arranged to make human life possible. Every one of the laws of physics, chemistry, and biology of the fundamental forces such as gravity, electromagnetic forces, and the details of the structure of atoms and elements of the universe has been precisely tailored so that human beings may live.

Q: What is zero Volume?
A: Means nothing.

Q: What is a four-dimensional world?
A: There are four dimensions to human life. These are the mind, the body, the inner world, and the external world. The inner world can take to the fourth dimension of spirituality,

Q: What existed before the Big Bang? And what force could have caused the great explosion that resulted in a universe that did not exist before?
A: Before the existence of the universe, there was neither matter nor energy. There was total emptiness alone the one breath, the God. There was neither existence nor nonexistence, neither death nor immortality. There was neither the sign of night nor day, it was total darkness. No sky, no space, no sound, and time. The temperature was zero, with no force or movements, no particles, no liquid, no energy and matter, a state of nothingness meaning the fundamental state of matter known as *Prakriti.* The cause of the Big Bang is unknown. New images from James Webb telescopes challenge the theory of the Big Bang.

Q: What are Quasars?

A: Quasars are nature's most extreme phenomena. They belong to a class of objects called active galaxies, which are galaxies with unusually active central regions. Active galaxies come in a variety of luminosities and other properties, with quasars on the end. A single, luminous quasar can outshine a thousand Milky Way-like galaxies, and yet all of this light emanates from a region not much larger than our solar system.

Q: What is a Black hole in space?

A: A black hole is a place in space where gravity pulls so much that even light cannot get out. Gravity is so strong because matter has been squeezed into a tiny space. This can happen when a star is dying.

Because no light can get out, people can't see black holes. They are invisible. Space telescopes with special tools can help find black holes. The special tools can see how stars that are very close to black holes act differently than other stars.

Q: The human population on earth has been increasing by millions over the years. How can this be explained in terms of rebirth

A: There are countless world systems in the universe known as Multiverse. The earth is an insignificant speck in the universe. It is not the only place where life exists. A being is born to a particular plane depending on his accumulated Karma. As per Buddha, the number of beings in the universe is so vast that it cannot be counted. Therefore, beings can be born from any of these planes into the human plane.

Q: Can humans be reborn as animals or trees?

A: Animals are emotional beings just like humans, comprised of mind and matter. They have consciousness to some extent but not to the limit of human beings. A being may be born in the animal plane which is classed below that of humanity as a result of his or her *Karma*. A plan consciousness is very limited, rebirth as a plant or tree may not be possible. However, as per Jainism, everything goes through the cycle of reincarnation.

Q: Why are there different religions if there is one God?

A: God is supreme and eternal. People from different cultures and religions have different concepts and faiths. There cannot be one religion due to the disparities between people. Their faith is rigid right from the beginning of their life depending upon the environment of the family. A person born in a Christian family is brought up a Christian. A similar situation is in the case of Hinduism and Islam. Every religion has a different concept of God. Water is the same but its name changes as per different languages. When people all over the world understand that all religions have the same concept of God, there would be heaven on earth.

Q: Which is the best religion?

A: All religions are best and preach morals and ethics. Choose one which is suitable for you. All roads emerge into one. Stay above religion and believe in spirituality. Love and respect people and their religions. Do not fight by religion. All people are children of God irrespective of their religions. He loves all equally.

Q; What should we do in life to please God?

A: God will repay everyone according to what they have done. To those who by patiently doing good seek glory, honor, and immortality, He will give eternal life. But for those who are self-seeking and who reject the truth and follow evil, there will be wrath and anger. There will be anguish and distress for everyone who does evil.

Q: What is the ultimate end of the universe?

A: Some say the world will end in fire, others say in Ice. Scientists think that the expansion of the universe ultimately makes it cool as it expands, and the universe may die. The entropy in an isolated system will continuously increase until it reaches a maximum value. At that point, heat in the system will be evenly distributed no room for usable energy (heat) to exist. Mechanical motion in the system will no longer be possible. This theory is named as Big Freeze theory which is also known as the Heat Death. Anyway, change is certain. This analogy resembles the concept of the creation of the universe in the oldest religion Hinduism. Rig Veda mentioned, the universe is a continuous cycle of creation and destruction. There is no beginning and there is no end.

Q: Are we alone in this universe?
A: Scientists are working throughout the world to find the presence of any intelligent life. There are some signs such as UFOs indicating the presence of aliens. However, there is not any concrete proof of life on any other planet.

Q: What is the Universe made of?
A: 95 % Dark matter and Dark energy. Both are invisible.

Q: How did life come to earth?
A: This is still unknown. A mystery of science.

Q: How big is the Solar System?
A: Solar system has a radius of 4.5 billion kilometers and a diameter of 9 billion kilometers.

Q: How big is the Universe?
A: Universe has a radius of 50 billion light years. Within this, our milky way has a radius of approximately 150,000 light years.

Q: Is there life elsewhere in the Solar System?
A: Scientists are searching for the possibility of life on Mars, and Moon but nothing can be said till now.

Q: Do we have a Volcano in our Solar System?
A: The largest Volcano in our Solar System is called Olympus Mons, located on the planet Mars. It is 25 km high.

Q: Do all the planets in the Solar System rotate in the same direction?
A: No. Most of the planets in our Solar System rotate in a counterclockwise direction except Venus and Uranus. They spin in opposite directions

Q: How old is our Solar System?
A: Although the Big Bang occurred 13.8 billion years ago, but our Solar System was formed 9 billion years later. So, our Solar System is 4.5 billion years old.

Q: What is the Solar System?
A: There are 8 different planets in our Solar System such as Mercury, Venus, Earth, Mars, Jupiter, Saturn, Uranus, and Neptune. All these planets orbit around one big star, the Sun.

Afterword

The Existence of God is not only a complex but controversial subject. The controversy between science and religion always goes hand in hand. Science is the only one and depends upon observations resulting in only one truth, whereas religions are many and based on their Holy scriptures revealing many myths. Old discoveries of science become myths when they are replaced by new discoveries. When modern science discovers anything, religions start claiming that it has been mentioned in their Holy scriptures a long time ago. Nothing is new, join the myths.

Science is objective whereas religion is subjective and depends upon faith. In a real sense, both depend on faith. Science believes that the universe is orderly and operates consistently according to a set of pre-ordained "laws of physics" and there is an intelligent operator. Science also trusts in the wisdom of scientists' observation and analysis. Science also believes in the accuracy of its instruments and mathematical theorem. Though there could be some variations among the observers too since they are human beings. Moreover, some scientific discoveries are also contradictory and often replaced by new ones. Nevertheless, chemical structures are imaginary, too. One can't observe them. The structure of simple benzene is assumed but never seen.

A Survey of the Holy Scriptures of all religions emphasizes the existence of God. Science also supports the existence of God through the theory of the Big Bang by saying there is a beginning of every universe or multiverse. If there is a beginning then there must be a Beginner, a supernatural, trans-physical being. Nothing comes from nothing. Had there been anything natural or physical out there, it would have been a part of the universe. So, it must be metaphysical. Moreover, the latest findings by the James Webb space telescope created doubt about the Big Bang theory as well.

Science further evidence for the fine-tuning universe is the confirmation of a supernatural and intelligent designer, The universe is too complex to have arisen by chance and cannot be so organized and in equilibrium.

It reminds me of the expression by Francis Collins, "I have found there is a wonderful harmony in the complementary truths of science and faith. The God of the Bible is also the God of the genome. God can be found in the cathedral or in the laboratory. By investigating God's majestic and awesome creation, science can actually be a means of worship."

It is not out of the way to mention Albert Einstein here, "Science without Religion is lame and Religion without science is blind."

"Science and religion are not at odds. Science is simply too young to understand."
— *Dan Brown,*

Bibliography

Adams F.C., and Laughlin, G. (2000). *Five ages of the Universe: Inside the Physics of Eternity,* A Touch Stone Book, Simon & Schuster, N.Y.

Alexander, E. (2012). *Proof of Heaven: A Neurosurgeon Journey into After Life*, Simon & Schuster, NY.

Ali, A. Y. (1983). *The Holy Quran*, Amana Corporation, Maryland, USA.

Aslan, R. (2017). *God: A Human History,* Random House, Division of Penguin, NY.

Bhayana, N. (2015). *Not Scared of God, but Man*, The Times of India, March 15.

Begley, S. (1998). *Science Finds God*, Newsweek, Inc.

Boa, K.D. and Bowman Jr. R.M. (2005). *20 Compelling Pieces of Evidence That God Exists*, David C. Cook, Second Ed., UK.

Braude, S. E. (2003). *Immortal Remains the Evidence for Life After Death*, Rowman and Littlefield Publishers, NY.

Capra, F. (1991). *The Tao of Physics,* Shambhala Publications, Boston. USA

Cayce, E. (2012). *Reincarnation & Karma*, A.R.E. Press, Virginia. USA.

Chalmers, D.J. (1996). *The Conscious Mind in Search of a Fundamental Theory*, Oxford University Press, NY.

Craig, W.L. (1996). *Cosmos and Creator, Origins & Design*, Spring, vol. 17, p. 19

Creighton, J. (2022). *Kardashev Scales,* Futurism. Com

Darling, D. (2022). *Kardashev Civilizations*, www.daviddarling.info

Das, R. (2012). *The Illustrated Encyclopedia of Hinduism.* Anness Publishing, Ltd. USA.

Davies, P. (1984). *Superforce: The Search for a Grand Unified Theory of Nature*, Penguin books, p. 184.

Dawkins, R. (2006). *The God Delusion*, Hughton Mifflin Company, Boston, New York.

Debroy, B. and Debroy D. (2011). *The Holy Vedas*, B.R. Publishing Corporation, India.

Dembski, W.A. (1999). *Intelligent Design,* InterVarsity Press, Illinois. USA.

Denton, M. (1998). *Nature's Destiny: How the Laws of Biology Reveal Purpose in the Universe*, The New York: The Free Press, p. 12-13.

Dimitrov, T. (2008). *"50 Nobel Laureates, and Other Great Scientists Who Believe in God,"* USA, e-book.

Doniger, W. (2004). *Hindus Myths: A sourcebook Translated from Sanskrit. (Penguin Classics).* Penguin Books, USA.

Dowson, J. (2000). *Classical Dictionary of Hindu Mythology and Religion: Geography, History.* DK Print World's Edition, New Delhi, India. Trubner and Company. Original Published 1879, Oxford University.

Ehrman, B.D. (2021). *Heaven and Hell: A History of the Afterlife*, Simon &Schuster, NY.

Flew, A. and Varghese, A.R. (2007). *There is a God*, Harper One, an Imprint of Harper Collins Publisher, New York.

Gandhi, H.K. (2010). *Theory of Karma in Eastern Religions,* Adhiatama Vigyan Prakashan, Ahmedabad, India.

Guillen, M. (2021). *Believing Is Seeing: A Physicist Explains How Science Shattered His Atheism and Revealed the Necessity of Faith,* Tyndale Refresh, Carol Stream, Illinois. USA.

Hackin, J. (1963). *Asiatic Mythology 1932,* Thomas Y. Crowell Company. USA.

Hartman, J. (1893). *The Creation of God,* The Truth Seeker Company, NY.

Hoyle, F. (1984). *The Intelligent Universe,* Holt, Rinehart and Wilson, NY, p. 184-185.

Jung, C. G. (1989). *Memories, Dreams, Reflections,* Vintage Books, NY.

Kansal, A. (2012) *"The Evolution of Gods,"* HarperCollins Publisher, India,

Kardashev, N.S. (1964). Transmission of Information by Extraterrestrial Civilizations, *Soviet Astronomy,* 8 (2).

Kung, H. (1980). *Does God Exist? An answer for Today,* English translation by Edward Quinn, Doubleday & Company, Inc. original in German and published by R. Piper & Company, Verlag, München, 1978.

Lanza, R., and Berman, B. (2010). *"Biocentrism,"* Benbella Books Inc., Dallas, Texas.

Lennox, J.C. (2021). *Cosmic Chemistry: Do God and Science Mix,* Lion Books, www.lionhudson.com, part of the SPCK Group, London.

MacLeod. A. (2010). *The Transformation- Healing your Past Lives to Realize your Soul's Potential,* Sounds True, Boulders, Colorado.

Martin, S.H. (2009). *The Science of Life After Death: The New Research Shows Human Consciousness Lives On*, Oakleaf Press, Richmond, Virginia.

Meyer S. (2010). *Signature in the Cell and the Evidence of Intelligent Design*, HarperCollins e-books, NY.

Meyer, S. (2021). *Return of the God Hypothesis: Three Scientific Discoveries that Reveal the Mind Behind the Universe*, HarperOne Publisher, NY.

Monroe, R. (1992). *Journey Out of The Body*, Broadway Books, NY.

Moody, R. (2015) *Life after Life*, HarperOne, an imprint of HarperCollins Publisher, NY.

Naskar, A. (2016). *"Love, God & Neurons: Memoir of a Scientist Who Found Himself by Getting Lost,"* An Amazon Publishing Company, USA.

Navabi, A. (2022). *Why there is no God*. Atheist Republic, USA.

O'Connell, M. (2016). *Finding God in Science*, Eigen Publishing, Orange County, California.

Pandey, R.C. (1999). *Surya Siddhanta*, Chaukhamaba Surbharati Prakashan, Varanasi, India.

Parnia, S. (2013). *Erasing Death: The Science That is Rewriting The Boundaries Between Life and Death*, HarperOne, an imprint of HarperCollins Publishers, NY.

Parnia, S. (2007). *What Happens when we Die*, Hay House Publisher, NY.

Puri, R. K. (2017). *Consciousness: The Ultimate Reality,* Authors House Publishers, Indiana, USA.

Puri, R.K. (2021). *Meditations Over Medications,* Authors House Publishers. Indiana, USA.

Rao, R. (2022). *Creation of the Universe: A Vedic Perspective,* Independently Published, India.

Ross, H. (1995). *The Creator and the Cosmos: How Greatest Scientific Discoveries of The Century Reveal God,* Colorado: NavPress, revised edition, 1995, p. 76.

Schultes, E., and Hofmann, A. (1979). *Plants of the Gods,* McGraw-Hill Book Company, New York.

Searle, J.R. (1992). *The Rediscovery of the Mind,* A Bradford Book, The MTS Press, Cambridge, UK.

Sehgal, V. (2010). *Creation vs Evolution,* Amazon kindle edition.

Sivananda, S. (1972). *What Becomes of the Soul After Death,* The Divine Life Society, India.

Weise, B. (1988). *Many lives, and Many Masters.* Simons & Schuster, N.Y.

Yahya, A. (2000). *The Creation of the Universe,* Al-Antique, Publisher Inc, Toronto, Canada.

Yogananda, P. (1946). *Autobiography of a Yogi.* Self-Realization Fellowship, LA, USA.

Young, P.J. (2014). *If there is a God, whose God is God?* Dr PaulYoungpublication.com.

Glossary of Terms

Advaita: Nondualism, one ultimate reality.

Ahamkara: Egoistic, arrogant, proud

Atman: Soul

Avatar: Descendent of God

Beingness: Condition of having existence

Biogenesis: Synthesis of substances by a living organism. Living matter arises only from living matter.

Brahma: The supreme power, God as creator

Brahma Kumaris: A spiritual movement. The organization is known for the prominent role played by women. They have 8500 centers in 100 countries.

Buddha: Awakened one, a title for one who has attained enlightenment.

Dharma: Religion

Ego-cons: Ego consciousness composed of mind, intellect, body, and consciousness

Karma: Actions

Koran: Sacred book of The Muslims

Lord Krishna: Avatar

Lord Rama: Avatar

Lord Vishnu: Preserver, God

Lord Shiva: Destroyer, God

Lepton: A lepton is an elementary, half-integer spin (spin/2) particle that does not undergo strong interactions. Two main classes of leptons exist charged leptons, also known as electron-like leptons, and neutral leptons (better known as neutrinos).

Maya: Illusion

Moksha: To get rid of the cycles of birth and death

Nag Loka: Snake world

Neti, Neti: Not this not that

Naraka: Hell

Nirvana: Extinction of selfish desire and selfish conditioning

Nirgun: without form

Prana: Life, is about breath. There are 5 types of pranas. Vyana (diffusion-pertaining to the nervous systUdanadana (ascending - throat, upper chest) Prana (inward moving - heart, chest lungs) Samana (equalizing - naval- digestion), and Apana (below the naval - excretory and reproduction).

Purana: Sacred text of Hindus, old scriptures

Patala Loka: Under the earth

Quarks: an elementary particle and a fundamental constituent of matter. Quarks combine to form composite particles called hadrons, the most stable of which are protons and neutrons, the components of atomic nuclei.

Saguna: with form

Samsara: Wheel of existence, the individual soul returns again and again to know various forms of embodiment

Samskaras: A deep mental impression produced by past experiences

Satya Yuga: Era, Golden period

Swarga Loka: Heaven

Tattva Brahma Assi: I am Brahma

Treta Yuga: Era, Silver Age

Upanishads: Upanishads are the Bible of Indians. There are 108 survived. The age of the Upanishad is unknown.

Vedanta: Philosophy of Vedas

Vedas: Holy literature of Hindus. There are four Vedas. Sam Veda, Yajur Veda, Athar Veda, and Rig Veda

Yoga: Union between the human soul and divine essence

Also, by
Ravi K. Puri
At AuthorHouse

Meditation Over Medication
Consciousness: The Ultimate Reality
Aphrodisiacs: Myth or Reality